vacationing with saddle & packhorse

vacationing with saddle & packhorse

BILL MERRILL

ARCO PUBLISHING COMPANY, INC.
219 Park Avenue South, New York, N.Y. 10003

Published by Arco Publishing Company, Inc., 219 Park Avenue South, New York, N.Y. 10003

Library of Congress Catalog Card Number 74-76828
ISBN 0-668-03486-6

Printed in the United States of America

To Horace Marden Albright, former Director of the National Park Service, one of the great conservationists of this century, who helped start and pioneer the National Park Service into the fine organization it is today, a man of integrity and understanding who loves the parks and forests . . . and who has done much for his country.

Foreword

Millions of Americans have already discovered and are visiting our great outdoors, and more are doing it every year. The National Parks, the National Forests and Grasslands, and other public lands afford a wide variety of outdoor recreation opportunities to young and old alike. The visitors come to hike, picnic, camp, ski, swim, fish, hunt, record sounds, take pictures, or simply to observe nature's many wonders. Most come by car to developed facilities, but more and more people are hiking or packing into the backcountry using saddle and packhorse outfits.

The American and Canadian sportsman is fortunate in having the opportunity to visit and to hunt and fish on large acreages of public land at relatively low costs. This opportunity does not exist in most countries.

The United States Forest Service of the Department of Agriculture manages the National Forest System for sustained yields of all its renewable resources: wood, water, recreation, wildlife habitats, and forage. Through multiple use land management, wildlife habitats are improved, with resultant increases in the numbers and quality of wildlife species. Recreation areas of many kinds are developed. Areas of wilderness—a concept first provided by the Forest Service in 1924—are a part of the National Forest Systems resources so important to Americans.

W. K. "Bill" Merrill's 40 years of experience as a Ranger and outdoorsman come through clearly in his new book, *Vacationing with Saddle and Packhorse.* His numerous tips and practical advice on safety, comfort, and care of stock show his respect for the great outdoor experience.

Edward P. Cliff, Chief, Retired
United States Forest Service

Contents

	Preface	11
	Acknowledgments	13
1	An Introduction to Vacationing on Horseback	17
2	Try a North American Safari This Year	41
3	Locations and Special Features of Wilderness Areas	55
4	Where to Write for Trail Ride or Pack Outfit Information	75
5	Start with a Walking and Burro Safari	95
6	The Technique of Burro Handling	105
7	Saddle and Packhorse Hunting Can Be Thrilling!	129
8	The Last Frontier—The Adventure of a Lifetime!	141
9	Boots, Saddles, Packs and Hitches	153

10	Trailside Camp Cookery—How to Eat Happily in the Woods!	179
11	First Aid if You Need It!	195
12	First Aid for Your Mount	198
13	Selecting a Saddle or Pack-horse—Rent or Buy?	215
14	The Care and Feeding of Horses and Mules—The Correct Way!	229
15	Miscellaneous Tips for New Horsemen	239
	Bibliography	259
	Appendix	263
	National Forests, Parks, Monuments & Recreation Areas	263
	National Forest Regional Headquarters Offices	289
	National Park Service Regional Offices	290
	Bureau of Land Management Land Offices	291
	Dealers and Outfitters	292
	Sources of Emergency Rations & Dehydrated Foods	296
	Index	297

Preface

Since my retirement after 36 years in the Ranger Service, many outdoor friends and officials in the recreation field have asked me to write a handbook on trail riding and vacation camping with saddle and packhorse outfit—a manual more comprehensive than the one or two chapters on the subject found in a few outdoor books. They wanted one that would cover the areas in which the once-a-season or once-in-a-lifetime camper, hunter, or fisherman and his family are not quite skilled, and also a book that would be interesting to the experienced horseman, too. Although comprehensive in scope, I realize that this book cannot cover every detail. For those of you who wish more information on all phases of training stock and horsemanship, a detailed bibliography is included.

Camping out on horseback is *the* new vacation trend. Wilderness travel is increasing rapidly each year, and has now reached a point in some of our National Forest and National Park areas where camping and grazing stock restrictions are necessary to protect some of the more heavily used areas from permanent damage. With this increase in backcountry use, it is more necessary than ever that all who visit the wilderness country assume their share of the responsibility in keeping these areas unspoiled and unmarked by stock and human use. This can be accomplished *only* if all of us work together toward this end.

This book will show you the way to plan a horseback safari, where to write for detailed information and maps, and how to water, feed, and care for your saddle and pack animals in the remote wilderness whether you rent or own your own stock—and how to do it in comfort and safety.

I hope that you will like this book, and that it will add to a new adventure and happy experience when you vacation with saddle and pack outfit far into the wild country of this great nation.

W. K. Merrill

Acknowledgments

The production of this handbook would have been much more difficult without the kind assistance of many specialists. The author wishes to acknowledge his deep appreciation to many Rangers, guides, packers, outfitters, organizations, officials, and dignitaries for their material, photographs, and comments, and whose suggestions contributed to the preparations of this vacation guide, and to:

Mr. Edward P. Cliff, Chief, United States Forest Service.

Mr. George A. Hartzog, Jr., Director, National Park Service.

Mr. Horace M. Albright, former Director, National Park Service.

Mr. Fred J. Overly, Reg. Dir. N. W. Reg. U. S. Bureau of Recreation.

Mr. A. P. Snyder, Dist. Ranger, High Sierra Dist. Sierra National Forest.

Mr. Joe Barnes, guide and packer, Mather Pack Station, Mather, California.

Mr. Joe Back, author and retired guide and packer, Dubois, Wyoming.

Mr. Glidden McNeel & Sons, guides and packers, Alpine Valley Ranch, Wyoming.

Mr. W. E. DeCarteret, DeCarteret Pack Trains, Sequoia–Kings Canyon National Parks.

Mr. Bill Guth & Sons, Outfitters and white water guides, Salmon, Idaho.

Mr. O. A. Cranny, Leavitt Meadow Pack Station, Bridgeport, California.

Mr. W. A. Stewart, Glacier Pack Trains, Big Pine, California.

Mr. Clyde Ormond, author, outdoorsman and conservationist, Bigby, Idaho.

Mr. Nicholas Roosevelt, author and conservationist, Big Sur, California.

Mr. L. S. Bergstrom, Doctor of Veterinarian Medicine, Sonora, California.

Mr. John Francis Lehman, TV Studio Prod. Mgr. WSYR, Syracuse, New York.

Mr. Albert Minton, Department of Commerce & Development, State of Idaho.

Mr. and Mrs. Dudley Boothe, Rainbow Pack Outfit, Bishop, California

Mr. and Mrs. Raymond Holmgren, Little Antelope Lodge and Pack Station, Colville, California.

Mr. Sally Weller, Flying W Ranch, Incorporated, Tionesta, Pennsylvania.

Mrs. Barbara Emerson, Exec. Sec. Editorial, *Western Horseman*, Colorado Springs, Colorado.

Mrs. Diana Murphy, Exec. Sec. Dept. of Economic Development, Anchorage, Alaska.

Mrs. Margaret Rose Merrill, Author and conservationist, Sonora, California.

Miss Alice Fryslie, Exec. Sec. Montana Outfitters and Dude Ranches, Helena, Montana.

Miss Josephine Brooker, Asst. Dir. Advertising Dept. Montana Highway Dept.

The California State Parks and Recreations Department, Resources Agencies.

The California Department of Fish and Game, Sacramento, California.

The United States Bureau of Recreation, Department of the Interior.

The United States Bureau of Land Management, Department of the Interior.

The United States Fish and Wildlife Service, Department of the Interior.

The Yosemite Park & Curry Company, Yosemite National Park, California.

The Yellowstone Park Company, Yellowstone National Park, Montana, Idaho, Wyoming.

The University of California Extension Service, Davis, California.

The American National Red Cross, Washington, D. C.

The Wilderness Society, Washington, D. C.

The National Rifle Association, Washington, D. C.

The Black Hills Trail Association, South Dakota.

The Illinois State Stock Horse Association, Chicago, Illinois.

The Royal Canadian Mounted Police, Ottawa, Canada.

The Sierra Club, 1050 Mills Tower, San Francisco, California.

Firearms International Corp.; Remington Arms Co.; Winchester Arms Co.

To each of these, and to the many others who have helped but are not mentioned, my sincere appreciation.

W. K. M.

Deep in the heart of the Canadian Rockies, the base camps of the Trail Riders and Skyline Trail Hikers depend on horses to bring in supplies. Camps are changed each year to allow riders and hikers to explore new wonders, far from the traveled routes of cars and trains. (Canadian Government Travel Bureau photo.)

1

An Introduction to Vacationing on Horseback

A Change of Pace Most of us are in a vacation rut: instead of returning refreshed and relaxed, we return from a summer's jaunt more tired and tense than the day we left. We tend to go to the same places and do the same things every vacation, year in and year out. To waste every season's outing in this manner is tragic when a world most of us have never thought of before lies open to us. If we change this trend we can see new sights, absorb new scents, and gain a better knowledge of the outdoors.

Our Wonderful Vacationland Outdoor recreation in our great scenic National Parks, Forests, Primitive and Wilderness recreational areas is increasing by leaps and bounds. Each year millions of people visit these vacation spots seeking rest and relaxation. This explosive increase in forest visitors is due to more leisure time, larger salaries, faster transportation, an ever increasing interest in the out-of-doors, and the proximity of many of these recreation areas to large population centers.

The New Trend Most of these teeming millions of vacationers crowd around the resorts and nearby water and boating areas. There is a way to get away from the vacationing masses: take a trail trek on horseback into the high country!

A New Thrill A thrilling experience awaits the family and individual who want to escape the ordinary. Away from a madly paced business world, the peace and quiet of the wild mountain country can only be reached on foot or by saddle and packhorse outfit. Getting away from the rush and noise of the city to nature's wild places is nature's sedative, offering healing for the weary metropolitan if he will take a camping trip deep into the high country on horseback!

Room to Roam From the arid deserts to the Arctic tundra, through all imaginable types of climate and terrain, there stretch thousands of square miles in the wilderness sections of our national parks and forests, plus the vast 718,698 square miles of public domain under the management of the Bureau of Land Management, Department of the Interior, mostly contained in 14 Western states and Alaska. Many Indian Reservations are also open to hunting, fishing, camping, and trail riding. This wide-open space offers an invigorating change from the hurry and press of urban life—refreshment for the spirit in its scenic grandeur.

What You Will See Here on a mountainside trail, halfway to heaven, another kind of contentment is yours: a buoyant well-being that springs from the clear pure air high among the snow-capped peaks of North America's mountains.

The Splendor of the Mountains Breathtaking coastal shores can be seen as you ride the trails along ranges. Inland mountain ranges provide yawning river chasms, luxuriant forests, snow-capped mountains, flower-draped alpine meadows, rolling rangeland, wilderness lakes, rippling trout streams, and big-game country inhabited by wildlife. This is the wilderness of the primeval forests: the province of wild creatures, the far retreat of man!

Many Ask What Is Wilderness? Please stand still a moment and listen! Here, in the silence of the mountains and forests, the stillness has sounds you will never hear in the loud, crowded labyrinth of the city.

In the quiet of the forest you can experience the rippling murmur of a wild river; the rustle of the wind through the trees; the pungent smell of pine and fir; the wary passage of a deer; the whisper of wild flowers waving in the breeze; the chattering of a squirrel; the hammering of a woodpecker; or the honking of high flying geese.

About the Wilderness Act Neither the Wilderness Act of September 3, 1964, nor statistical data can explain to the average person what a primitive or wilderness area is, or why it is so important. A colored map tells little of the actual back-of-beyond country or its effect on people who visit it. Those who know and have traveled deep into the wilderness need no explanation; those who do not know find only a hint in the printed word and in pictures.

The essence of a wilderness is the experience that one derives from its special environment. To some extent wilderness is a link with our heritage of the frontier, but it is also a discovery or renewal of something within us. You might call it an aloneness, a detachment from normal cares and responsibilities, and a renewed feeling of one's place in nature. In the wilderness one finds not only recreation, but an opportunity for recreation of mind, of body, and of spirit. Here the visitor is on his own, and he makes his own pleasure and comfort or his own trouble and discomfort.

To every man wilderness is a personal experience that adds a new dimension to his character. So that people may always discover this experience, which has no substitute, wilderness has been set aside.

People discover wilderness in many places and in many ways. For some it may be just a day's ride through a forest in North Carolina, or a week's pack trip in Oregon's Three Sisters Wilderness. Others may explore the rugged vastness of the Selway-Bitterroot or Bob Marshal Wildernesses of Montana, or trail ride in the desert in search of the Lost Dutchman Mine in the Superstition Wilderness of Arizona. Still others trailer their saddle horses south for a trail ride in the Anza-Borrega Desert State Park in California.

Fun for the Nimrod and Angler Good hunting and fishing are found in most wilderness areas, all of which are open in season under State laws. Clear lakes and pure streams provide excellent fishing in most regions. Within the wilderness are whitetail, blacktail and mule deer, elk, bighorn sheep, mountain goat, javelina (desert wild pig), and bear, plus many species of small animals and upland game birds. For the scientist and nature student, the geology and ecology of these remote places guarantee many hours of fascinating study. The wilderness is a photographer's delight, and for everyone there is solitude in the midst of unparalleled, unspoiled scenery.

High Adventure—Frontiersman Style For those who know the land, these areas evoke the names of famous frontiersmen; Coronado, Daniel Boone, Davy Crockett, Lewis and Clark, Jim Bridger, Jed Smith, Chief Joseph, Cochise, John Muir, and many others who blazed the trails across our country and gave color and substance to our wilderness history.

Fishing, camping, boating, photography or sightseeing? You can enjoy your favorite vacation recreation in Colorado's year-round playground at Top of the Nation.

Rediscovering Old Trails We can now rediscover this old-fashioned style of travel. Horseback vacation camping recreates the experience of the early explorers and settlers in their journey across the nation. Modern trail riders are finding early blazed trails that are again resounding with the pounding of horse's hooves instead of the rubber tires of modern vehicles.

The First Horses, Mules, and Burros The first horses, mules, and burros were brought to North America by the Spanish conquistadores to conquer and pillage Mexico. De Soto is known to have abandoned some of his stock in what is now known as Texas. These and other strays were to be progenitors of the wild burros and mustangs which were so abundant on the western plains a century later, and which gave the American Indians mounts for the first time.

Two decades after his first attempt, De Soto landed in Florida with more men and horses. Later the heavier horses of the English and French mixed with the Arabian species of the Spanish, and soon men and horses moved westward starting saddle and packhorse transportation in the New World.

Shortly after World War II the Army gave up horse transportation, and the number of horses in this country began to decline. Added to this was the indiscriminate killing of wild horses and burros in the Southwest for fox and mink food. Fortunately, public opinion put a stop to this needless slaughter, and in the past decade these animals came back strongly, and their number is now increasing rapidly from year to year.

One must not forget that four-legged animals can go where all mechanical means of transportation fail, and in all kinds of weather. These beasts of burden will continue to be man's surest means of transportation in wild terrain, especially in our wilderness recreational areas.

The Return of the Horse The horse has survived modernization! After World War II, there was a slowdown in horse breeding; however, that has now changed as thousands of city people moved to suburban and rural areas on the edge of large cities and purchased one or more acres so that they could have a horse or two in their corral.

It is no secret that over the past 15 years there has been a constant growth in the number of registered horses of all breeds. Along with this increase, several new "breed" associations have been formed, some of which have to do with color of horses, and others with origin by countries or peculiarities of gait.

Chief among the "new" breeds over the past decade has been the Quarter Horse. No breed in the history of this country has increased in numbers so rapidly as has the Quarter Horse.

The Light Breeds All together, according to a survey taken by a private commercial organization and the U. S. Department of Agriculture, it is estimated that in the United States alone the horse population is now over nine million animals, not counting the several million horses and mules in Canada and Mexico.

The greatest number of these are what are called "light breeds," meaning riding, racing, show, rodeo, trail, and pack stock.

Coupled with this great increase in horses has been the growth of a number of publications (both books and magazines) that deal with all breeds, their training and horsemanship.

Because of this increased interest in equestrian sport, including trail riding and packing into the wilderness country for family camping, fishing, and big-game hunting, there has been a great demand for equestrian care. Colleges and universities are graduating over 20,000 veterinarians each year. The demand has been so great that many colleges are even giving courses in corrective horse shoeing. So far there just don't seem to be enough farriers!

Los Angeles Goes All Out! The City of Los Angeles has recognized the horse as a major recreational factor for all ages, rich or poor. The new $7,200,000 Los Angeles Equestrian Center, a 75.2 acre portion of Griffith Park, is just a short canter from downtown. It is the only equestrian center of its kind in the world. However, several other cities are looking into the situation and will probably work along these lines for their areas. The centers will be self-supporting.

An outstanding feature of this trend is the opportunity the center offers the underprivileged. There are educational movies about equine anatomy, horsemanship, and the care and feeding of the horse. Officials at the center are going into the less affluent areas and bringing children to the center and giving them a chance to learn about horses, and letting them ride free of charge. Youngsters who appreciate and enjoy horses rarely, if ever, end up in Juvenile Hall.

4-H Clubs from the area put on horse and livestock shows in the center's big arena. As a matter of fact, every weekend is crowded with major and minor events, and many horse organizations from all over the nation put on horse shows at the center.

Our friend the horse has finally trotted into the status he deserves: as one of the officials states, "right into the hub of the city of motorized mayhem!"

The Circle Route One way to find out if there is a place nearby where you and your family can saddle up for a vacation on horseback is to use your town or city as a hub, and draw a circle out from it on an automobile map. One hour's driving time will take you out fifty miles and a two hour drive will take you one hundred miles, etc. Somewhere within one of these circles you will probably find a place that will take you out on a Trail Ride for a fee.

There Is Variety You can enjoy a pack outfit safari along the sky trails of the Rocky Mountains, the High Sierra Nevadas of California, the Coastal Ranges, the flat prairie lands of the Midwest in the 19 Grasslands of the National Forests, or the beautiful old mountains of the Eastern States.

Many horseback treks take the vacationer to areas of the North American Continent that could never be viewed from a freeway or town lot. For example, there are parts of the country in wilderness areas that are still unexplored, and on maps they are shown as vacant white spaces marked *unsurveyed!* The vast Selway and Bob Marshal Wilderness Areas of Idaho-Montana contain hundreds of square miles of rugged mountains, canyons, and alpine lakes and meadows which are open only to travelers who are willing to leave motorized and mechanical means of transportation behind and travel in the manner of the pioneer of yesteryear.

Why is there a longing felt by many city dwellers to ride a horse and hit the trail for the beckoning back-country? It's hard to explain. Perhaps it is a latent instinct brought out in those who have visited and savored the beauties of one of our national parks or forests. Here one can enjoy vast vistas of beautiful scenery, fighting trout in wild whitewater streams with deep pools, camping in an alpine meadow decked with wild flowers near crystal clear lakes surrounded by towering mountains that poke their heads into the blue sky

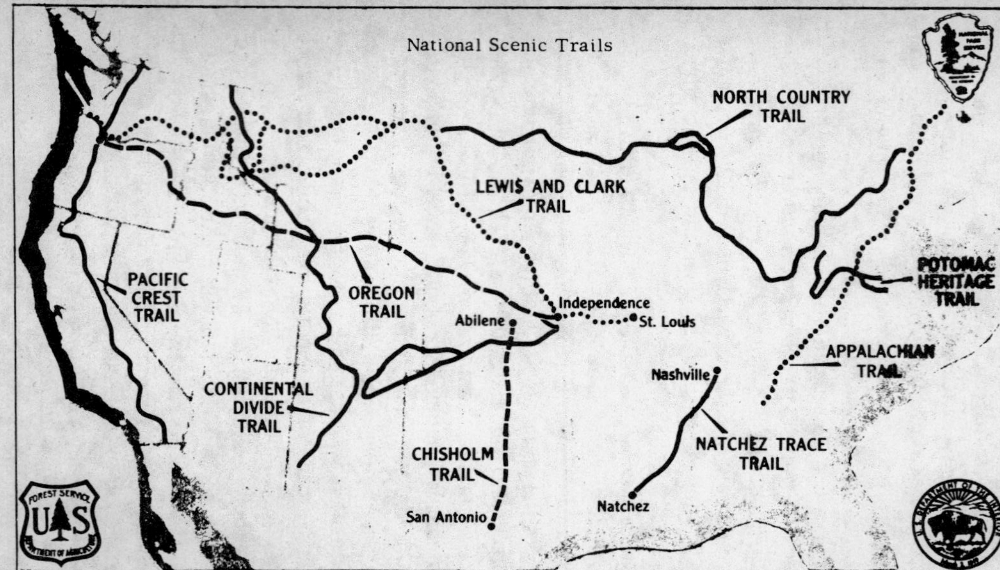

National Scenic Trails.

through fluffy white cumulus clouds. At night the sky is filled with millions of sparkling stars that look as though you could reach out and touch them. Above all, there is a feeling of peace and tranquility and a release from the hostilities of life and urban cares!

The National Scenic Trail System It would take the trail rider and pack outfitter a lifetime to travel over the new trail system. Two long trails, the 2,050 mile long Appalachian Trail running through several National Parks and Forests from Maine to Georgia, and the famous 2,400 mile Pacific Crest Trail that travels from the Canadian border to the Mexican border are the first trails established in the New National Scenic Trail System.

Potential Additions to the National Trail System The Continental Divide Trail is 3,100 miles long, and the Potomac Heritage is 825 miles. The Old Cattle Trails of the Southwest are over 1,600 miles. The Lewis and Clark Trail, follows both the outbound and inbound routes of the Lewis and Clark Expedition, running from Wood River, Illinois to the Pacific Ocean in Oregon. Natchez Trace meanders some 600 miles from Nashville, Tennessee to Natchez, Mississippi. The great North Country Trail snakes 3,200 miles from the Appalachian Trail in Vermont, through New York, Pennsylvania, Ohio, Michigan, Wisconsin, and Minnesota, to join the Lewis and Clark Trail in North Dakota. The Oregon Trail will travel 2,000 miles from Independence, Missouri to near Fort Vancouver, Washington. The old Sante Fe Trail runs 800 miles from Independence, Missouri to end at Sante Fe, New Mexico. The Vermont Long Trail is short: 255 miles from the Massachusetts border through Vermont to connect with trails at the Canadian border. The Old Mormon Trail will go from Nauvoo, Illinois, through Iowa, Nebraska, and Wyoming to Salt Lake City, Utah. A system of Gold Rush Trails is proposed for Alaska. The Mormon Battalion trail will run some 2,000 miles from Mount Pisgah, Iowa, through Kansas, Colorado, New Mexico, and Arizona to Los Angeles, California. All this is in the offing for the hiker and trail rider!

Horseback Riding in the National Park System

Whether you sit tall in the saddle or short, you can view the wonders of the National Park System to advantage from horseback or muleback. The National Park Service operates 6,591 miles of well-marked trails for equestrian use, and 70 miles of carriage trails.

A journey into the depths of Haleakala volcano at Haleakala National Park, Hawaii, offers an assortment of thrills. Guided tours range from 12 to 30 miles, providing one to four days of outdoor fun in a balmy climate. Glimpses of rare birds and an abundance of exotic plant life offer rewarding dividends. The trip descends toward the colorful lava flows of the dormant volcano.

Glacier National Park in Montana provides 875 miles of wilderness trails. Two-hour tours, as well as longer expeditions, take riders into the midst of spectacular mountain scenery.

At Grand Canyon National Park, Arizona, mules are often the most feasible method of transportation. Seeming to defy gravity, mules are better equipped than horses to handle this terrain, which drops some 3,000 feet from the Canyon rim to the Colorado River. Trips last seven hours to two days, depending on the rider's preference and durability. Tours are conducted from May 15 through September 30.

Riding is a major recreational activity in 49 of the 260 authorized areas of the National Park System. Concessions, stables, or ranches furnish trips through such diverse scenery as mountains, seashores, deserts, forests, and lake and river country. Riders visit historic and archeological sites. Most areas permit only guided tours.

Visitors who enjoy range riding on their own may do so at Badlands National Monument, South Dakota; Dinosaur National Monument, Colorado; Arches National Monument, Utah; Organ Pipe Cactus National Monument, Arizona; Arbuckle Reservoir, Oklahoma; and Curecanti Recreation Area, Colorado.

Both trail riding and range riding are offered at Theodore Roosevelt National Memorial Park, North Dakota. Riders at Canyon de Chelly National Monument, Arizona, accompanied by guides, can ride along the canyon's scenic rim or onto the sandy floored canyon among the Navajo sheepherders.

In Grand Canyon National Park, the Havasupai Indian village in Havasu Canyon is a popular objective of the more rugged riders. Reservations must be made by telephone or letter to the Tourist Manager, Havasupai Tourist Enterprise, Supai, Arizona, who will send a guide to meet you some 67 miles northeast of Peach Springs, Arizona. You ride an Indian pony eight miles down into the canyon. The Supai serve no meals and you must take in your own fuel and stove. There is a packhorse limit of 150 pounds.

In Yellowstone National Park, the visitor can take stagecoach rides over Sagebrush trails along the Yellowstone River. Two stagecoaches operate from June 18 to August 28. In Mesa Verde National Park, an old-fashioned hayride behind a spirited team of horses has proved popular.

Group expeditions on horseback are common in many areas of the National Park System. Trail riding associations specialize in pack trips into the back country. A person could ride a couple of hundred miles every summer on National Park System trails for 30 years without going over the same trail twice.

Forty-one areas provide trails, mostly west of the Mississippi River. Two Eastern parks, Acadia National Park, Maine, and Blue Ridge Parkway, Virginia-North Carolina, permit horseback riding on certain carriage roads.

Trail mileage ranges from one mile at Coulee Dam National Recreation Area to 1,110 miles in Yellowstone National Park. Five National parks—Glacier, Yellowstone, Olympic, Sequoia-Kings Canyon and Yosemite—each have 500 or more miles of horse trails. Eight areas —Glacier, Rocky Mountain, Yellowstone, Crater Lake, Sequoia-Kings Canyon, Yosemite National Park, and Devils Postpile National Monument—are traversed by two proposed National Scenic Trails, the Pacific Coast Trail and the Continental Divide Trail.

There is a wide variation in the availability of horses and facilities from area to area. You can generally rent a horse by the hour, day, week, month, or season. In 35 areas, concessioners provide saddlehorses with experienced guides. Grand Teton National Park, Wyoming, for example, has 200 horses available at its Jenny Lake concession, and 100 to 150 available at Jackson Lake. Some areas provide no rentals or stables but permit riding by visitors able to furnish their own mounts and provisions.

The wide, open spaces are not the only popular riding areas. One way to enjoy a visit to Washington, D. C. is to take advantage of some 20 miles of riding trails through Rock Creek Park and along Potomac Parkway. The Rock Creek and Rock Creek Valley (Edgewater) Stables have 92 horses, and most patrons take one hour rides. Rock Creek Stable is open year around and allows the more experienced rider to go out without a guide. Edgewater offers guided tours only, but both stables offer instruction. Rock Creek Stable has three-gaited horses only.

Horseback riding is one of the oldest recreations in the 95 year history of the National Park System. Horses were once a necessity if one wanted to see the wonders of the first national park, Yellowstone National Park, established in 1872. When President Chester A. Arthur decided to see Yellowstone in 1883 he did so by pack trip, with General Phil H. Sheridan as one of his camp-mates. The riders covered 350 miles in 24 days.

President Theodore Roosevelt was another avid horseman in national park areas. One park he explored on horseback is Grand Canyon National Park, which he set aside as a national monument in 1908. The visitor can retrace the horseback routes of the Presidents today at Yellowstone and Grand Canyon.

Eight areas of the National Park System east of the Mississippi River offer horseback riding: Acadia National Park, Maine; National Capital Parks, Washington, D. C.; Blue Ridge Parkway, Virginia-North Carolina; Chickamauga and Chattanooga National Military Park, Georgia-North Carolina; Great Smoky Mountains National Park, North Carolina-Tennessee; Hot Springs National Park, Arkansas; Natchez Trace Parkway, Mississippi-Tennessee-Alabama; and Shenandoah National Park, Virginia.

West of the Mississippi, in the northerly mountains, you can ride in four national parks: Yellowstone, Wyoming-Idaho-Montana; Rocky Mountain, Colorado; Grand Teton, Wyoming; and Glacier, Montana; three national monuments: Badlands, South Dakota; Colorado, Colorado; and Dinosaur, Utah-Colorado; two national recreation areas, Curencanti and Shadow

Mountain, Colorado; plus Theodore Roosevelt National Memorial Park, North Dakota.

In the Southwest there is horseback riding in seven national parks: Bryce Canyon, Canyonlands and Zion, all in Utah; Big Bend, Texas; Grand Canyon, Arizona; Mesa Verde, Colorado; Platt, Oklahoma; and in nine national monuments: Arches and Rainbow Bridge, Utah; Canyon de Chelly, Chiricahua, Grand Canyon, Navajo, Saguaro, and Organ Pipe Cactus, all in Arizona; and Bandelier, New Mexico. There is also riding at Arbuckle Reservoir, Oklahoma.

In California, the rider may choose from trails in four national parks: Yosemite, Sequoia-Kings Canyon, and Lassen Volcanic; three national monuments: Death Valley, Devils Postpile, and Joshua Tree; plus Point Reyes National Seashore. In Oregon, Crater Lake National Park has riding trails. In Washington there is riding at Olympic and Mount Rainier National Parks, and at Coulee Dam Recreation Area. Both of Hawaii's national parks, Haleakala and Hawaii Volcanoes, provide riding trails.

When to Go In the summer at family vacation time or in the fall when colors are at their best. Normally the high mountain passes are not clear of snow until the middle of July, and some passes are not clear until later.

The National Forests Trail System There are approximately 165,000 miles of hiking and riding trails in the national forests. As the Nation's recreational development increases, this mileage will undoubtedly increase, particularly in the wilderness areas.

In the East there is the over 2,000 mile long Appalachian Trail, extending from Mount Katahdin in Maine to Springer Mountain in Georgia. Almost one-third of this great trail winds through eight National Forests

Riders and pack string on Minnows Creek Trail near its junction with John Muir Trail in the John Muir Wilderness Area, Sierra National Forest, California. (U.S. Forest Service photo.)

with foot and horse trails spreading out in all directions. For maps, information, and guide service write the Appalachian Trail Conference, 1718 N Street, N.W., Washington, D. C. 20036.

In the West there is the great Pacific Crest Trail System, which stretches over 2,400 miles from the Canadian border to the Mexican border, traverses 19 national forests—with about 1,500-miles in National Forests Wilderness. With lateral foot and horse trails extending east and west, plus the 1,150-miles of the California Hiking and Riding Trail System added along the coast range of California, this mass of trails is a bonanza for trail riders. The nation will soon be criss-crossed from East to West and North to South when the National Scenic Trail System gets fully underway!

The Difference Between National Parks and National Forests It still appears that some newspaper reporters (and much of the public) are confused regarding these two agencies. Both play an important part in the lives of the people of our nation, but millions of people visit these areas without realizing that there is a definite distinction between the two kinds of reservations.

The following explanation will show you their differences:

National Park System

The National Park System consists of 290 natural, historical and recreational areas of national significance. These areas range from Alaska to the Virgin Islands and from Puerto Rico to Hawaii. The Department of the Interior's National Park Service administers 278 areas. The remaining 12 are managed under agreement with the Service.

The National Park Service was established by Congress in 1916 "to promote and regulate the use of the . . . national parks, monuments and reservations" in accordance with their purpose which "is to conserve the scenery and the natural and historic objects and the wild life therein . . . by such means as will leave them unimpaired for the enjoyment of future generations."

In 1964 the Secretary of the Interior recommended separate management concepts for the "three different categories of areas, natural, historical and recreational." On January 1, 1968 there were 67 Natural Areas, 165 Historical Areas, and 30 Recreational Areas in the National Park System, plus the National Capital Parks, the park system of the Nation's Capital.

The Natural Areas comprise 38 national parks, 34 national monuments and Ice Age National Scientific Reserve, Wisconsin. The Historical Areas range from Mesa Verde National Park to Statue of Liberty National Monument and Gettysburg National Military Park. The Recreational Areas include national recreation areas, such as Lake Mead National Recreation Area, national parkways, national seashores, national lakeshores and Ozark National Scenic Riverways.

Congress established the first national park in 1872 when it set aside more than two million acres as Yellowstone National Park at the junction of Wyoming, Montana, and Idaho; about 95 percent of the park is in Wyoming. Yellowstone is still the largest of our 33 national parks, often called the "crown jewels" of the National Park System for its superlative scenery, wildlife and wonders of nature. The largest area in the System is Glacier Bay National Monument, Alaska, which contains 2,803,840 acres. The smallest area is the House Where Lincoln Died which occupies one-twentieth of an acre opposite Ford's Theatre in Washington, D. C.

More than 140 million visitors were recorded in National Park System areas in 1967. The annual attendance is expected to exceed 300 million by 1976.

The national park idea, an American concept first expressed in the establishment of Yellowstone National Park, has been adopted by more than 90 nations. The National Park Service actively assists other countries throughout the world in establishing and expanding national park programs.

National Forest System

The National Forest System comprises 155 National Forests and 19 National Grasslands in 41 States and Puerto Rico. These public lands are administered by the Forest Service, U.S. Department of Agriculture.

As directed by Congress, renewable forest resources —water, timber, forage, wildlife, recreation—are managed under the principles of Multiple Use and Sustained Yield. Multiple Use means that resource management is coordinated so that areas of land produce a combination of values that best serves the American people. Sustained Yield means that resources are managed so as to provide services and products at a level of supply as high as can be sustained without harming the land's ability to produce. Under such management, the National Forests represent the Nation's largest tangible accomplishment in forest resource conservation.

Water from the forests irrigates millions of agricultural acres and is used for domestic and industrial purposes in hundreds of cities. Timber from the forests is manufactured into 5,000 products sold worldwide. National Forests and Grasslands provide habitat for millions of big and small game, game birds, and fish, and produce forage for 1,300,000 cattle and 2,600,000

Wilderness Patrolman advises a visitor on the proper route of travel and care of the wilderness country in the Sawtooth Primitive Area, Sawtooth National Forest. (U.S. Forest Service photo.)

sheep. Forest recreation includes scenic drives, wilderness travel, picnicking, camping, hiking, skiing, swimming, boating and, subject to State conservation laws, some of the country's finest hunting and fishing. The National Forests are truly America's Playgrounds.

The Forest Service pioneered in wilderness preservation in 1924 when it set aside the Nation's first Wilderness. The initial 9.1 million acres of the National Wilderness Preservation System created in 1964 are in 54 National Forest Wildernesses, previously classified as Wilderness, Wild, and Canoe Areas. Another 5½ million acres of the National Forests, set aside in 34 Primitive Areas, are being studied for possible inclusion in the wilderness system.

The Forest Service has two other equally important responsibilities. It maintains eight regional forest and range experiment stations, an Institute of Tropical Forestry, an Institute of Northern Forestry, and a Forest Products Laboratory. It also directs programs to encourage and support better management and protection of forest lands in State and private ownership.

Your Hosts—The U. S. Park Rangers, Forest Rangers, and State Game Wardens These men are a combination of many things, whether they serve in the high mountains and tall timbered country or in the rolling grasslands. They are the law, public educators, information bureaus, rescuers, wildlife protectors, fire fighting directors, repairmen, researchers, recreation counselors, and general jacks-of-all-trades. Most are men with a college background in forest management, wildlife management, geology, botany, recreation, law enforcement, or some other natural science. They are devoted to outdoor life and must possess great physical stamina and mental maturity. They have been trained to make quick and intelligent decisions at the right time, and to carry out these decisions with great skill based on an experienced understanding of the outdoor environment and the creatures who live there. They are in the forests and mountains to do a job—to protect you and to protect the wildlife and forests. Meet them halfway! They are friendly people!

Single file, the Trail Riders of the Canadian Rockies pick their way along unfrequented tracks, surrounded by the majestic untouched beauty of mountains, valleys, lakes and streams seldom visited by white men. Two clubs, the Trail Riders and the Skyline Trail Hikers, hold five camps each summer, in different locations each year. (Canadian Government Travel Bureau photo.)

2

Try a North American Safari This Year

A Mountain Safari With the possible exception of a wilderness canoe trek through the lake country of the north woods, a jaunt of one or more weeks into wild mountain country with a saddle and pack horse outfit is the ultimate in North American vacations. In fact there is nothing more satisfying than to recall a successful safari deep into the mountains, no matter whether it was planned to get away from the cares of civilization, or just in the need of a change of pace—to do something different or take a hunting or fishing outing away from competition. In any event, the trip will bring you many fine memories as the years pass by, memories of the tinkling of grazing bells near camp as the horses crop sweet meadow grass, of fish caught in some remote alpine lake, or of the big buck deer brought back for the home freezer to be shared with friends. Memories of the fragrance of whispering pine and fir, the aroma of camp coffee, the smell of frying bacon, and of the tall tales told around the sparkling campfire with fine companions will come back to you. As time passes on, you can relive the experience, and share the trip with friends who were not so fortunate, by showing them your slides or movies of the safari.

The matchless variety of things to do and see, combined with magnificent scenery and ideal climate, make a pack trip vacation a romantic experience to be cherished for a lifetime.

Two Kinds of Rides There are two types of horseback vacations: pack trips and trail rides.

Should You Take a Spot Trip? A spot trek, or for that matter any pack jaunt, requires no special equipment, just the usual camping gear you take on your automobile camping trips. If you don't own camp gear, you can rent or purchase what is needed. Don't borrow it if you can help it!

One-Day Spot Trip This is one of the more economical pack trips. On a one-day spot trek, you furnish all your own equipment and food, as the pack outfit is just a means of transportation. You will mount your horse (or riding mule if you prefer) at the pack station or corral at the end of the road-head for your ride into the back-country, and your camping gear, food, and camp comforts will be packed on sturdy pack animals. You will be guided to a predecided camp, usually at a scenic campsite on the edge of an alpine meadow, lake, or bend of a stream, and generally in excellent hunting and fishing terrain. After unloading the stock, your packer and the animals will return to the pack station while you get organized and set up your camp fly or canvas home away from home. In this case you are only charged for the day you are packed in and the day you are packed out. Don't forget, you feed the packer on all the trips!

Two-Day Spot Trip Longer trips to more remote areas necessitate the packer and stock staying overnight and returning to headquarters the following day. Your return trip will also require two days service from the packer and stock. When the pack train returns for you on the stipulated date, it will be the end of your vacation safari into the mountain forest holiday. The economical spot trip is the most popular type of trip and is used by many families, hunters, and fishermen. You will have had a grand adventure with days to fish, hike, explore, snap pictures or take movies, read, paint, observe wildlife and look at alpine flowers, or just loaf and relax in the sun.

The All-Expense Jaunt Of course, this is a more expensive way to head for the hills. However, this is a favorite with the office-soft professional man, as well as with families that can afford this type of travel. Your food is furnished and cooked for you (you can furnish a menu list or the outfitter will send you a list of food he will take). The camping equipment is provided, except your personal gear. All you need to bring are your personal effects: a warm sleeping bag, air mattress, fishing or hunting gear (don't forget the licenses), camera, binoculars, and comfortable walking shoes since you can't stay in the saddle all the time. Riding or cowboy type boots are not comfortable for walking very far!

The Extended Pack Safari In the traveling or extended safari, the stock and packer remain with you for the duration of the trip. You can choose to make a central or base camp and take daily trips from there, or you can plan to move camp every few days into another area. Each group brings all its own equipment and provisions. When making out your menu, remember you will have an extra mouth or two to feed: the packer or guide plus any extra hands such as a cook or horse wrangler, and any guest that you invite along the trail to join you in a meal.

Extended trips are especially popular with those who enjoy seeing new country, like to ride, plan to visit more lakes and streams, enjoy exploring new places, and want to photograph the beautiful and unusual.

The Dunnage Pack For those who like to walk, but don't wish to carry their gear, the dunnage pack is a good idea. A dunnage pack is often used by confirmed hikers and backpackers, especially if they feel they are not acclimated to their packs and the elevation. In this case, the packer loads your gear on a pack animal and will leave it at a designated spot while you hike up to your camp at your leisure. This arrangement can be made for your out-trip or you can backpack out. Many young people save money this way, using it is a means of getting the bulk of their gear into the high back-country so they can then proceed to backpack further out from their camp using their pack frames.

A dunnage pack trip is often the initial pack for persons who wish to gain experience in backpacking. Backpack jaunts from a base camp will help determine what is important to take, how to save weight, and how to refine and go light.

For large groups such as Boy and Girl Scouts, and church, YMCA, YWCA, and other organizations, a dunnage pack trip is an economical and ideal way to travel the Sky Trails. The group can have their gear spotted at a base camp, or retain the packer and stock to carry the weight while everybody hikes along care-free and unencumbered to a new campsite.

The Walking Pack Trip Some pack stations have burros or walking horses or mules (they poke along at a comfortable walking pace) that they will allow you to take with you if you are experienced in the care of pack animals, and that means correct watering, feeding, packing, and the responsibility that goes with the animals.

Burros are delightful, if at times obstinate, creatures, and they make fine pets. Families especially enjoy the attention and antics of these sometimes exuberant beasts, and children love them. For a leisurely and enjoyable trek, burros are worth considering.

Don't Forget the Time Element! Serious consideration should be given to the fact that it takes time to take care of your animal(s). You have full responsibility for them, which includes seeing that they have proper and sufficient water and feed and that they do not stray off and leave you afoot miles from the pack station. This will probably entail climbing out of the sack early each morning to hunt for and tend the stock. Always check with your outfitter as to how the animals are to be tended; whether they are to be picketed, turned loose, or hobbled and turned out. (See burro trips later on in the book.)

How About Backpacking? Once you are packed into a base camp, you might want to backpack or rock climb. This is an enjoyable way to see high country not negotiable by four-legged animals. If you rock climb, be sure that you are experienced, and never climb alone. Proper planning of food, equipment, and clothes is essential for your welfare. The prime requisite is keeping the weight down in your pack. There are many excellent dehydrated foods on the market that will help you conserve on weight.

If You Only Have a Few Days to Spend in the Hills In addition to the areas you can visit using your car, you can find pack train stations or corrals at most road heads in the mountains. You will be able to obtain horses there for a day's ride into the backcountry, or to

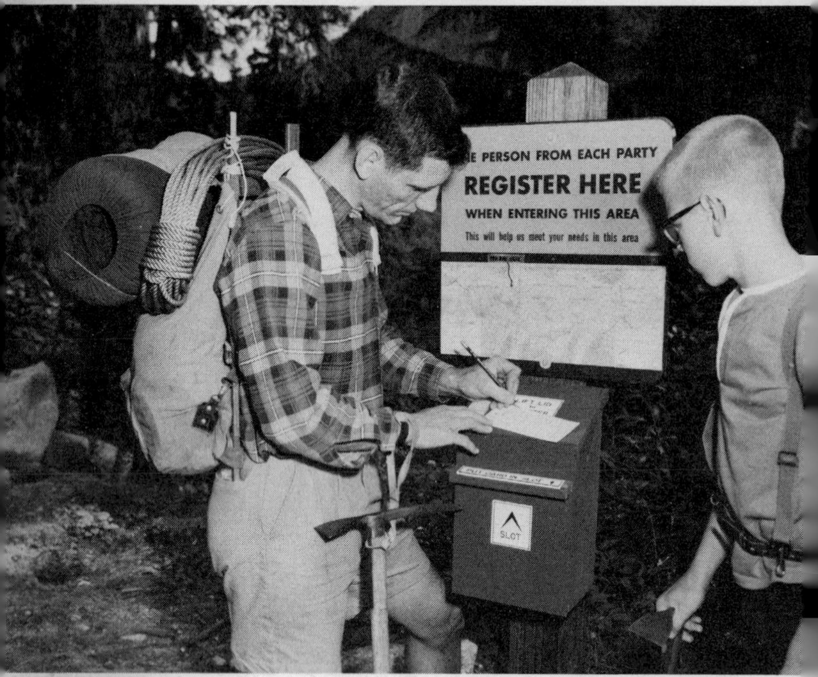

Mountain climbers Dewey Huston and his son Mike, of Bellingham, Michigan, write in the information requested at a registration station on Wilderness Trail No. 674, Mt. Baker National Forest, Washington. (U.S. Forest Service photo.)

explore the local forest trails for a few hours, or perhaps to join an organized ride with a group of people. A day trail ride will give you a taste of what you will enjoy on your entire proposed pack safari later on.

You might enjoy leaving your automobile at one of the road ends, then hiking leisurely up the trail, carrying your camera, lunch, and fishing gear. You are sure to enjoy the day if you take it easy.

Trips Are Really Tailored to Each Individual Yes, the pack outfitter will arrange to give you whatever type of safari you prefer or whatever combination appeals to you. If you have any questions or problems, don't hesitate to consult your packer, for each and every outfitter wants your high country safari to be the best vacation you ever had!

What Will My Backcountry Safari Cost? Of course, the type of trip you take will depend on family finances. Each area varies in type of terrain and distance to be traveled to the desired campsite, so that prices may be slightly high in one location and low in another. Don't forget to add car, air, or rail travel to the town where the outfitter will pick you up. The following prices are an example only of cost from the pack station. Remember that average costs are subject to changes from year to year.

Spot Trip

For a campsite two to four hours riding time from the pack station, the average total round trip would be $40.00 per person. For more remote campsites of five to seven hours riding time, the cost would be $75.00 for the round trip per person. The length of your stay does not affect the cost.

Extended Trip

Average cost (based on a party of four) would be $20.00 per day for each member of the party.

All-Expense Trip

Average cost (based on a party of four) would be $30.00 per day for each member of the party.

Dunnage Pack

Charges are for packer and each mule required. Average cost for one packer and using one mule would be $25.00 with an additional $6.00 for each mule used. (Average load—150 pounds per mule, limit of 5 mules per packer.)

Day Trips

There are various types of day rides. Obtain saddle stock without guide—$6 to $8 per day. Guide for your party—$15.00 per day and up. Organized group rides—$3.00 to $5.00 and up, as cost will vary with length and type of ride.

The following is an example of a price sheet you might receive from one of the pack outfits. Many packers list only stock prices instead of spot trip rates.

Horses	$ 7.00	per day
Mules	7.00	per day
Packer	25.00	per day
Cook	20.00	per day

Using these figures, you could figure the cost of your trip. For longer spot trips, double the total below:

A spot trip for a party of five to a campsite taking four hours of riding for a stay of ten days (the length of your stay does not affect the price):

5 saddle horses in @ $7.00 each	$35.00
5 mules in @ $7.00 each	35.00
1 packer in @ $25.00 each	25.00
Cost for your trip in would be	$95.00

5 saddle horses out @ $7.00 each	$35.00
3 mules out @ $7.00 each	21.00
1 packer out @ $25.00 each	25.00
Cost for your trip out would be	$81.00

Total cost for your round trip is $176.00. So the trip would cost $35.00 per person, plus your share of the food and car transportation. Once you have packed into the mountains, you can't spend any money as there isn't any store around the corner. This is one of the many reasons why a pack trip has become the ideal family vacation.

Tips for Pack Trippers Your packer will generally repack the gear you brought in kyacks or panniers. However, he will greet you with open arms if you arrive with your equipment properly packed and balanced in 50-pound packages or in your own kyacks. There are usually not enough saddlebags to go around, so it is a good idea to bring your own, either canvas or leather ones. Clothing and other personal items should be packed in strong waterproof canvas duffel bags. Bottled goods should be wrapped in newspapers or shirts or other soft cloth and placed in the center of the bag to prevent breakage. Remember, items you use often should be packed so that you can get to them without having to dig down to the bottom of the pack. The following tips will be helpful:

How Many Mules Will I Need?

An average mule load is 150 pounds and in most parties it works out that a mule per person is sufficient for a seven day stay. This allows you to camp in normal comfort.

To Help You and Your Packer

In order to save time and unnecessary correspondence, please give the following information in your first letter to the packer:

1. How many persons will there be in your party?
2. Approximately what dates will you want to pack in and pack out?
3. To what lakes or to what area do you wish to pack?
4. Can you estimate how large your pack load will be—how many pounds?
5. Will you want continuous hire of the packer or animals, or will you want a spot pack trip?

The usual procedure is to make your reservation early to insure stock for the dates you prefer. Leave explicit instructions with those back home as to where you're going and how you can be contacted.

Rules of the Trail

A pack tripper—

1. Properly prepares for his trip—sufficient food,

good sleeping facilities, first aid kit, proper clothes and equipment. Planning ahead leaves you free to enjoy your trip.

2. Uses good common sense—be careful while camping or hiking—you may be many miles from the nearest doctor. A safe vacation is a happy vacation.
3. Never pollutes the streams or lakes by any means. If no toilet facilities are provided, he emulates the cat by digging and burying.
4. Does not destroy or remove Forest or Park Service trail signs or take short cuts on the trail (cutting switchbacks damages the trails and saves neither time nor effort).
5. Obeys Forest Service or National Park rules (Example: Pets and firearms are not permitted in the National Parks).
6. Remembers that stock have right-of-way on the trail. Stands quietly off the trail until the stock has passed.
7. Clears the ground of any combustible material before building a fire, checking to see if the flames might ignite the branches above. NEVER leaves a fire unattended and when leaving extinguishes the fire—checking with the hand to be certain that no heat remains.
8. Leaves his camp cleaner than he found it. Cuts the lids off of his cans, burns and crushes them and packs them back out with him. DOES NOT bury his cans and refuse.

The Western Pack Station Few people realize the large number of pack stations and strings still operating in Western United States, Canada, and Mexico. Nor do they realize the short season outfitters have—plus an investment of anywhere from $50,000 to over $200,000. This not only includes horses and mules averaging $150 to $200 or more per animal, but riding and pack saddles, bridles, halters, blankets, pack harness, ky-acks, panniers, canvas mantys, rope, horse shoes, nails, hay, grain, pasturage, pack station and general camping equipment, plus wages for cooks, guides, and horse wranglers. Transportation is another expensive item, and often requires jeeps, trucks, boats, and aircraft to get a client from the nearest town or railhead or from the home ranch and to haul stock and equipment to the end of the road or jump-off point. Packers have to charge enough to make a go of it. Many don't.

The Primitive Backcountry Fortunately, much of the Western part of the North American Continent still contains vast areas of primitive wilderness that pack trains can still travel in, where the penetration of motorized conveyance is prohibited by law, or where the area is impossible to reach by road. There are extremely rugged mountain regions that bar the use of anything but the staunchest pack strings. Most pack stations cater to family groups, the once-a-year trail rider who wants to get away on a different kind of vacation, the fisherman after hungry trout who wants to get away from competition, or the hunter after a record game animal.

The Sure-Footed Mule It is difficult for this old Ranger to understand why some outdoor writers state that mule and burro use is almost exclusively confined to desert regions. This just is not true! Admittedly, in parts of Mexico and the Southwest, mules and burros are often favored in the arid sections to move freight to remote camps and mines. Due to their small size, burros place third in desert and mountain travel.

Mules are still used as pack animals and occasionally as saddle animals in the Northern Region, Beaverhead National Forest, Montana. This camp tender working for the Matador Company in Upper Ruby uses mules to move the sheep herders' teepee to a new location each night. (U.S. Forest Service photo.)

Mules and Burros in Wetlands Mules *are* used in the sometimes very wet Pacific Northwest by both the U. S. Forest Service and National Park Service. Mules are even packed by Rangers and trail crews in Olympic National Park's Rain Forest where the average rainfall is 12 feet! Trail crews in my Northwest Ranger district have at times used burros to pack their camps from one location to another. Granted, due to their smaller hooves, these animals are at times difficult to handle when fording streams or traversing boggy terrain, but so are horses at times! You just have to out-smart them!

Some packers prefer mules for packing. The mules being bred today are generally smarter than most pack-horses (and sometimes more stubborn). For a time the mule supply was almost non-existent. Now there seem to be a growing number of mule breeders attempting to supply a still growing demand. Due to rough terrain, the Forest and Park Service operations and many pack station owners preclude the use of any but the toughest and hardiest of animals.

The Riding Mule The riding mule is on its way back, according to The American Donkey and Mule Society. They make excellent saddle animals, and more and more of them are seen along the foot paths and high country trails. Grand Canyon National Park uses hundreds of them. In and around Bishop, California, for an example, over 1,000 are used on the east side of the Sierra Nevada Range.

3

Locations and Special Features of Wilderness Areas

Vacationing in Wild Country Using a modern definition, a trail ride or a pack trip is a camping trip on horseback into woods and mountain country that would be impossible to reach in any other way, except by walking. You can use a train, bus, commercial aircraft, or private transportation to reach some sort of starting point to enter the wilderness, but once you are there you are on your own and will rough it more-or-less, simply by doing without some unnecessary luxuries.

In this wild environment, there are no roadside parks with electricity and flush toilets, no screaming sirens and streams of roaring and honking traffic, and incidentally, no empty or broken bottles, cans, and wrapper debris. And the big surprise is that you will realize that it's not as tough a proposition as you probably thought it would be, and you will enjoy every minute of it!

A Pack Safari Can Be an "Escape Vacation" If camping beside a crystal clear lake amid towering snow-capped mountains, miles and miles from any hint of civilization appeals to you, then make it a point to hit the trail this summer.

If you seek out the wilderness, the remote spot belongs only to you and to the wild animals, far removed from the roar and dirt of the city, the crowded beaches, overfished streams, overflowing and confused campgrounds with blaring radios, honking car horns, dust, and shrieking kids, you will find the simple pleasure most of us are inclined to forget except when we are alone or with good friends.

If your longing is for the rugged peaks, quiet forests, blue lakes, and cascading streams of the primitive places, you will have joined the ranks of the elite in pleasure vacation camping!

NATIONAL FOREST PRIMITIVE AREAS
JANUARY 1, 1965

ARIZONA—422,990 acres

Name of wilderness	National Forest	Forest headquarters	Area (acres) Gross	Net	Special features
Chiricahua	Coronado	Tucson	18,000	18,000	On the crest of Chiricahua Mountain Range with precipitous scenic canyons radiating from the summit. Among the game species is the rare Chiricahua squirrel, found only in this vicinity.
Galiuro	Coronado	Tucson	55,000	55,000	Knifelike mountains jutting out of the Arizona plain. Extremely steep slopes limit travel to constructed trails. For experienced travelers there is good hunting.
Mazatzal	Tonto	Phoenix	205,346	205,000	Precipitous topography containing many geological formations. Wildlife, but no fishing.
Sierra Ancha	Tonto	Phoenix	20,850	20,850	Precipitous mountains. Prehistoric and Pueblo Indian cliff dwellings. Varied vegetation and wildlife.
Superstition	Tonto	Phoenix	124,140	124,140	Extremely rough with occasional prominent peaks. Replete with mining folklore of the Southwest, particularly from the prospecting days.

CALIFORNIA—1,256,884 acres					
Caribou	Lassen	Susanville	19,080	19,080	A wild mountainous area of volcanic origin near Mt. Lassen in Northern California. Attractive small lakes with good fishing and some wildlife.
Cucamonga	San Bernardino	San Bernardino	9,022	9,022	Gentle to rugged topography reaching maximum altitude of 8,911 feet. Habitat of deer and mountain sheep. Challenging to hikers, with rewards of exceptional views.
Dome Land	Sequoia	Porterville	62,561	62,121	Picturesque domes and spires of bare rock. Elevations from 3000 to 9529 feet. Traversed by the precipitous South Fork of Kern River Canyon. Virgin forests cover some 6,000 acres.
Hoover	Inyo Toiyabe	Bishop Reno, Nevada	9,000 33,800 42,800	9,000 33,800 42,800	Rugged canyons & jagged peaks approaching 13,000 feet. Mountain lakes & cascading streams. Meadows carpeted with spring flowers. Abundant wildlife, fishing, and remnants of 5 glaciers.
John Muir	Inyo Sierra	Bishop Fresno	230,217 274,046 504,263	228,932 274,046 502,978	Spectacular Sierra Crest country with elevations up to nearly 14,500 feet at Mount Whitney. Hundreds of lakes and streams, many with native golden trout. John Muir Trail traverses much of area. Wildlife, vegetation, and geologic features in abundance.

Marble Mountain	Klamath	Yreka	214,543	213,283	Outstanding mountain scenery of two types: the Marble Mountains of white and gray marble, and high granitic peaks to the south. A wide variety of tree species. Both stream and lake fishing.
Minarets	Inyo Sierra	Bishop Fresno	61,508 48,051 109,559	61,433 48,051 109,484	Rugged peaks and spires of unusual grandeur. One of finest climbing regions in the Sierra Nevada. Many streams, nearly 400 lakes, and about 25 remnants of glaciers.
Mokelumne	Eldorado Stanislaus	Placerville Sonora	41,560 8,840 50,400	41,560 8,840 50,400	High granite crest zone. Rugged and sparsely timbered. Abundant wildlife. Lake and stream fishing.
San Gorgonio	San Bernardino	San Bernardino	34,718	33,898	San Gorgonio Peak, 11,485 feet; desert to alpine scenery and vegetation.
San Jacinto	San Bernardino	San Bernardino	21,955	20,565	Mountains, meadows, and flats atop precipitous cliffs rising high above the Palm Springs desert country.
South Warner	Modoc	Alturas	69,547	68,507	A ridge 15 miles long, most of it over 9,000 feet in elevation. Numerous peaks, small meadows, and lakes. Summer range for mule deer.
Thousand Lakes	Lassen	Susanville	16,335	15,695	Peaks of volcanic origin and lava flows. Several timber-bound fishing lakes; scenic grandeur.
Yolla Bolly-Middle Eel	Mendocino Shasta-Trinity	Willows Redding	73,876 37,215 111,091	72,916 36,135 109,051	Variety of rugged scenery. Abundant wildlife. Good stream fishing in early part of season.

COLORADO—274,859 acres

Name of wilderness	National Forest	Forest headquarters	Area (acres) Gross	Net	Special features
La Garita	Gunnison Rio Grande	Gunnison Monte Vista	26,300 22,700 49,000	26,300 22,700 49,000	Along the Continental Divide with peaks exceeding 14,000 feet. Abundance of wildlife in an alpine and subalpine setting. Fishing in all streams and lakes.
Maroon Bells-Snowmass	White River	Glenwood Springs	66,280	66,100	Includes Snowmass Mountain, Maroon Bells, and Pyramid Peak, all over 14,000 feet high. Mountain sheep summer and winter at Conundrum Hot Springs. Excellent fishing.
Mount Zirkel	Routt	Steamboat Springs	72,180	72,180	Rough, scenic country astride the Continental Divide, Mt. Zirkel, 12,220 feet in elevation, is the highest peak. Many lakes and streams with good fishing. An elk summer range.
Rawah	Roosevelt	Fort Collins	26,797	25,579	In Medicine Bow Range. Includes a small glacier and numerous glacial lakes. Part of area is exceptionally rugged. Good fishing.
West Elk	Gunnison	Gunnison	62,000	62,000	Embraces parts of several high mountain ranges. Open park ranges, lakes and rushing streams. Summer range of many deer and elk.

IDAHO—987,910 acres					
Selway-Bitterroot[1]	Bitterroot Clearwater Nezperce	Hamilton, Mont. Orofino Grangeville	165,168 265,580 558,431 989,179	164,946 265,580 557,384 987,910	Mountainous wooded area lying mostly west of the Bitterroot Range. Wildlife and vegetation of great variety.
MINNESOTA—886,673 acres					
Boundary Waters Canoe Area	Superior	Duluth	1,034,852	886,673	The finest canoe country in America with hundreds of lakes ideal for canoeing. Excellent fishing in more remote regions. Largest wilderness east of the Rockies.
MONTANA—1,482,567 acres					
Anaconda-Pintlar	Beaverhead Deerlodge Bitterroot	Dillon Butte Hamilton	72,526 45,398 41,162 159,086	72,526 44,115 41,162 157,803	A scenic chain of high, barren, precipitous peaks along the Continental Divide. Forested slopes flank the crest. Many lakes and streams.
Bob Marshall	Flathead Lewis & Clark	Kalispell Great Falls	710,000 240,000 950,000	710,000 240,000 950,000	A spectacular mountain area with a wide variety of flora and fauna. Outstanding elk hunting and cut-throat trout fishing. Of great geologic interest, especially the "Chinese Wall."
Cabinet Mountain	Kaniksu Kootenai	Sandpoint Libby	39,663 54,609 94,272	39,663 54,609 94,272	A lofty, peak-studded area of scenic grandeur. Big game and wild flowers in abundance.

[1] Area is also in Montana.

[2] Area is also in Idaho.

Gates of the Mountains	Helena	Helena	28,562	28,562	Spectacular limestone cliffs and other geologic formations. Of interest relating to Lewis and Clark expedition.
Selway-Bitterroot[2]	Bitterroot Lolo	Hamilton Missoula	244,470 10,010 254,480	244,150 7,780 251,930	Mountainous wooded area lying mostly west of the Bitterroot Range. Wildlife and vegetation of great variety.

NEVADA—64,667 acres

Name of wilderness	National Forest	Forest headquarters	Area (acres) Gross	Net	Special features
Jarbidge	Humboldt	Elko	64,827	64,667	Rugged mountainous terrain with 8 peaks over 10,000 feet. Deer plentiful, small game and birds numerous. Good fishing in streams and one lake. One of the most scenic and remote spots in Nevada.

NEW HAMPSHIRE—5,400 acres

Great Gulf	White Mountain	Laconia	5,400	5,400	A rough, rugged mountain basin on the slopes of Mt. Washington. Accessible by trail. Elevations from 1,700 to 5,800 feet.

NEW MEXICO—678,661 acres

Gila[3]	Gila	Silver City	438,626	638,360	Topography rough to precipitous. Many deep box canyons. Good hunting and trout fishing.

Pecos	Carson Santa Fe	Taos Santa Fe	25,000 140,000 165,000	25,000 140,000 165,000	High back country with trout lakes and streams; elk and deer hunting.
San Pedro Parks	Santa Fe	Santa Fe	41,132	41,132	A high mountain plateau. Dense stands of spruce and open meadows with small trout streams. Deer, turkey, and grouse hunting.
Wheeler Peak	Carson	Taos	6,051	6,051	Outstanding scenery. Includes Wheeler Peak, elevation 13,160 feet—highest in New Mexico.
White Mountain	Lincoln	Alamogordo	28,230	28,118	A variety of mountain scenery and forest cover types. Elevation 6,000 to 11,000 feet.
		NORTH CAROLINA—21,055 acres			
Linville Gorge	Pisgah	Asheville	7,655	7,655	Deep, rough gorge with cascades, virgin timber, and flowering shrubs. Elevation ranges from 1,000 to 4,000 feet.
Shining Rock	Pisgah		13,400	13,400	Unique vegetation cover surmounted by Shining Rock Mountain of white quartz. Many waterfalls and springs. Outstanding deer and bear population. Good stream fishing.

[3] Gila Primitive Area partially reclassified in 1953 as wilderness, but some of the Primitive Area remained in primitive status.

OREGON—662,847 acres

Name of wilderness	National Forest	Forest headquarters	Area (acres) Gross	Net	Special features
Diamond Peak	Deschutes Willamette	Bend Eugene	19,240 16,200 35,440	19,240 16,200 35,440	Straddles the summit of the Cascade Mountains. Includes snow-capped Diamond Peak, 8,750 feet elevation, and 33 lakes. Occasional small mountain meadows adjacent to the lakes.
Eagle Cap	Wallowa-Whitman	Baker	220,280	216,250	Embraces some of the highest peaks and best fishing waters in eastern Oregon. Many geological formations. Elk, deer, bear, and lesser wildlife species are common.
Gearhart Mountain	Fremont	Lakeview	18,709	18,709	Spectacular "Gearhart Notch," rock palisades, good hunting and fishing. All local timber types are represented on the slopes.

OREGON—Continued

Name of wilderness	National Forest	Forest headquarters	Area (acres) Gross	Net	Special features
Kalmiopsis	**Siskiyou**	Grants Pass	78,850	78,850	Rough, steep mountainous area 500 to 5,000 feet in elevation. Noted for unusual plants and trees, including Kaliopsis leachiana and seventeen species of conifers. Abundant wildlife and good fishing.
Mountain Lakes	Winema	Klamath Falls	23,071	23,071	Mountain lakes within a bowl formed by eight prominent peaks. Elevations range from 5,000 to 7,950 feet. Abundant wildlife and good fishing.

Mount Hood	**Mount Hood**	Portland	14,160	14,160	Occupies the high country north and west of the summit of famous Mt. Hood. Outstanding examples of alpine meadows and living glaciers surround the peak.
Mount Washington	**Deschutes**	Bend	8,625	8,625	Straddles the summit of the Cascade Mountains. Includes snow-capped Mt. Washington, Little Belknap and Belknap Craters. Vast lava beds of recent origin, open glades and varied alpine timber types.
	Willamette	Eugene	38,030	38,030	
			46,655	46,655	
Strawberry Mountain	**Malheur**	John Day	33,653	33,004	Occupies the most rugged area in the John Day country. Seven high mountain lakes, alpine meadows, unique rock formations, and varied timber types.
Three Sisters	**Deschutes**	Bend	59,875	59,875	Includes the Three Sisters Mountains. Numerous peaks and glaciers, among them Collier glacier, Oregon's largest, on North Sister. Area contains 111 lakes.
	Willamette	Eugene	136,833	136,833	
			196,708	196,708	
WASHINGTON—583,196 acres					
Glacier Peak	**Mount Baker**	Bellingham	213,100	212,850	Outstanding for its many glaciers, numerous lakes, and alpine scenery. Glacier Peak is the central attraction. More than 30 peaks rise (up to 8,000 feet) above intervening valleys.
	Wenatchee	Wenatchee	254,405	245,255	
			458,505	458,105	
Goat Rocks	**Gifford Pinchot**	Vancouver	59,740	59,740	Extremely precipitous peaks. Glaciers, several large lakes, and great profusion of mountain flora. Mountain goats abundant.
	Snoqualmie	Seattle	22,940	22,940	
			82,680	82,680	

Mount Adams	Gifford Pinchot	Vancouver	42,411	42,411	Largely above timberline; spectacular "Around the Mountain" trail.
WYOMING—1,812,012 acres					
Bridger	Bridger	Kemmerer	383,300	383,300	In the Wind River Range. Elevations from 8,500 to 13,785 feet on Gannett Peak, the highest in Wyoming. Massive granite outcrops. Hundreds of lakes and picturesque streams provide excellent fishing. Noted for mountain climbing and live glaciers.
North Absaroka	Shoshone	Cody	359,700	359,700	Includes glaciers, natural bridge, standing petrified trees. Excellent hunting and fishing.
South Absaroka	Shoshone	Cody	506,300	505,552	Fishhawk Glacier; deep, straight-walled canyons. Back-country pack horse trips.
Teton	Teton	Jackson	563,500	563,460	Region of high plateaus, large valleys, and mountain meadows, easily traversed. Includes Two Ocean Pass, where Two Ocean Creek divides and sends its water to the Pacific and to the Atlantic. Noted for elk hunting and fishing. Summer range for Jackson Hole elk herd.

Name of Primitive Area	National Forest	Forest headquarters	Area (acres) Gross	Net	Special features
ARIZONA—250,936 acres					
Blue Range[1]	Apache	Springerville	181,566	180,139	Traversed by the Mogollon Rim with spruce and fir in the high country above and ponderosa pine in the broken country below. Big game is abundant.
Mount Baldy	Apache	Springerville	7,400	7,400	On northeast slope of Mt. Baldy at the head of the West Fork of Little Colorado River. Elevation to 11,496 feet.
Pine Mountain	Prescott	Prescott	8,530	8,530	Moderately rough terrain along Verde Rim. Big-game hunting good but difficult because of heavy cover and steep canyons.
	Tonto	Phoenix	8,970	8,915	
			17,500	17,445	
Sycamore Canyon	Coconino	Flagstaff	22,305	21,207	Includes a good representation of the canyon types of flora and fauna of northern Arizona. Spectacular geological formations.
	Kaibab	Williams	5,950	5,807	
	Prescott	Prescott	18,975	18,938	
			47,230	45,952	
CALIFORNIA—563,152 acres					
Aqua Tibia	Cleveland	San Diego	26,760	25,995	California's southernmost classified area. Contains unusual unburned virgin brush type.
Desolation Valley	Eldorado	Placerville	41,383	41,343	Extremely rough, rugged and alpine in every respect. Elevations from 6,500 to 10,020 feet.

[1] Area is also in New Mexico.

Devil Canyon-Bear Canyon	Angeles	Pasadena	35,267	35,267	Area of deep canyons 40 miles by road from Los Angeles.
Emigrant Basin	Stanislaus	Stanislaus	98,043	97,020	Includes many lakes, fine fishing, high granite topography.
High Sierra	Sequoia Sierra	Porterville Fresno	7,040 5,960 13,000	7,040 5,960 13,000	Extremely rough mountainous area, possibly the most truly wild in California. Includes Tehipite Valley, which approaches the scenic scale of Yosemite Valley. Great variety of vegetation and life zones. Monarch Divide is rough terrain with few travel routes.
Salmon Trinity Alps	Klamath Shasta-Trinity	Yreka Redding	34,556 251,200 285,756	28,576 194,724 223,300	A region of scenic beauty, including granite peaks, many alpine lakes, and numerous streams teeming with trout.
San Rafael	Los Padres	Santa Barbara	74,990	74,458	Embraces main range of San Rafael Mountains.
Ventana	Los Padres	Santa Barbara	54,857	52,769	Area of low elevation but rugged terrain.
		COLORADO—554,283 acres			
Flat Tops	White River	Glenwood Springs	117,800	117,800	Rolling, rock-rimmed plateau dotted with ponds. Summer range for the noted White River migratory deer and elk herds.
Gore Range-Eagle Nest	Arapaho White River	Golden Glenwood Springs	32,400 28,875 61,275	32,379 28,825 61,204	Spectacular knife ridges and pinnacles of the Gore Range are superlative rock-climbing terrain.

San Juan	San Juan	Durango	240,000	238,080	The Needle Mountains challenge rock climbers from all States. The San Juans abound in wildlife. Includes a Grizzly Bear Management Area. Large expanses without trails.
Uncompahgre	Uncompahgre	Delta	69,253	53,252	Extremely rugged mountains. Lakes and waterfalls. Wildlife is varied and abundant.

COLORADO—Continued

Name of Primitive Area	National Forest	Forest headquarters	Area (acres) Gross	Net	Special features
Upper Rio Grande	Rio Grande	Monte Vista	56,600	56,600	Adjoins the San Juan Primitive Area along the Continental Divide at the headwaters of the Rio Grande. Noted for trout fishing.
Wilson Mountains	San Juan	Durango	9,600	9,600	Includes 5 mountains and 2 major peaks of the Wilson Range. Large and small game in considerable numbers.
	Uncompahgre	Delta	17,747	17,747	
			27,347	27,347	

IDAHO—1,642,388 acres

Name of Primitive Area	National Forest	Forest headquarters	Gross	Net	Special features
Idaho	Boise	Boise	226,778	223,996	Rugged, scenic, and mountainous with towering peaks and deep canyons. Embraces the Middle Fork of Salmon River, noted for float boating and fishing. Excellent hunting. Large herds of deer and elk. Bighorn sheep common along the river.
	Challis	Challis	74,670	74,293	
	Payette	McCall	689,712	685,336	
	Salmon	Salmon	241,584	240,951	
			1,232,744	1,224,576	

Salmon River Breaks	Bitterroot	Hamilton, Mont.	122,500	122,500	Good hunting and fishing. More than 40 miles of frontage on the Salmon River. Rugged terrain and beautiful scenery. Adjoins Idaho Primitive Area.
	Nezperce	Grangeville	94,685	94,370	
			217,185	216,870	
Sawtooth	Boise	Boise	144,300	144,300	Scenic terrain featuring the Sawtooth Mountains. Numerous deep gorges and glacial basins, 170 alpine lakes. Fishing good to excellent. Noted for wildlife—deer, elk, mountain goat, bear, mountain lion, small game.
	Challis	Challis	7,900	7,900	
	Sawtooth	Twin Falls	48,742	48,742	
			200,942	200,942	
MONTANA—417,140 acres					
Absaroka	Gallatin	Bozeman	64,000	64,000	High mountain area, mainly wooded. Lofty peaks. Very good fishing; fair hunting, especially for moose.
Beartooth	Custer	Billings	175,000	175,000	Rugged high mountain area. Includes Granite peak (highest in Montana) and Grasshopper Glacier.
	Gallatin	Bozeman	55,000	55,000	
			230,000	230,000	
Mission Mountains	Flathead	Kalispell	75,500	73,340	High mountainous area of alpine lakes and peaks, containing glaciers and unique glacial evidence. Grizzly bear and mountain goat plentiful.
Spanish Peaks	Gallatin	Bozeman	50,00	49,800	Wild, moderately rough topography. Outstanding fishing.

NEW MEXICO—335,424 acres					
Black Range	Gila	Silver City	169,984	169,196	Rough, forested terrain. Good trout fishing and hunting, including the best deer and bear hunting in New Mexico.
Blue Range[2]	Apache	Springerville, Ariz.	36,598	36,598	Traversed by the Mogollon Rim with spruce and fir in the high country above and ponderosa pine in the broken country below. Big game is abundant.
Gila[3]	Gila	Silver City	132,788	129,630	Topography rough to precipitous. Many deep box canyons. Good hunting and trout fishing.
OREGON—86,700 acres					
Mount Jefferson	Deschutes Mount Hood Willamette	Bend Portland Eugene	25,710 3,470 57,520 86,700	25,710 3,470 57,520 86,700	Snow-capped Mt. Jefferson, 10,495 feet, second highest peak in Oregon. Perpetual glaciers and Three Fingered Jack are the main features of this Cascade summit area.

[2] Area is also in Arizona.

[3] Gila Primitive Area partially reclassified in 1953 as wilderness, but some of the Primitive Area remained in primitive status.

UTAH—240,717 acres

Name of Primitive Area	National Forest	Forest headquarters	Area (acres) Gross	Net	Special features
High Uintas	Ashley	Vernal	166,794	166,794	The High Uinta Mountains, ranging from 8,000 to 13,449 feet, are the highest in Utah and the only major east-west range in the United States. A wild, picturesque region, rich in scenic, geological, and biological interest. Noted for its small lake fishing in over 250 lakes.
	Wasatch	Salt Lake City	73,923	73,923	
			240,717	240,717	

WASHINGTON—801,000 acres

Name of Primitive Area	National Forest	Forest headquarters	Area (acres) Gross	Net	Special features
North Cascade	Mount Baker	Bellingham	434,200	434,200	An area to satisfy the demands of the most strenuous wilderness seeker, where he can travel for months without retracing his steps.
	Okanogan	Okanogan	366,800	366,800	
			801,000	801,000	

WYOMING—586,000 acres

Name of Primitive Area	National Forest	Forest headquarters	Area (acres) Gross	Net	Special features
Cloud Peak	Bighorn	Sheridan	137,000	137,000	The glacial sculpture of the Bighorn Range left near-vertical walls 1,000 to 5,000 feet high. Numerous lakes and remnants of glaciers near Cloud Peak and Blacktooth Mountain.

Glacier	Shoshone	Cody	177,000	177,000	Extremely rugged topography. Includes Fremont Peak, innumerable alpine lakes, and some of the largest living glaciers in the United States.
Popo Agie	Shoshone	Cody	70,000	70,000	Extremely rough topography along the Continental Divide. Contains 75 lakes; rich in historical lore.
Stratified	Shoshone	Cody	202,000	202,000	A region of narrow valleys and broad, flat-topped mountains, built up of lava flow. Rich in petrified forest remains. Abundant game.

On the trail in the Sawtooth Wilderness Area, Idaho. (U.S. Forest Service photo.)

4

Where to Write for Trail Ride or Pack Outfit Information

Trail Ride or Pack Outfit? First let me tell you a little about them, their costs, and where to write for free maps and detailed information.

There are two types of horseback vacations that are most popular: trail rides or packhorse jaunts. Trail rides are less demanding. You can bring your own horse, rent one, or obtain a mount at a dude ranch. Camps are usually made at easily accessible sites, or in an area where a chuck-wagon can be driven and equipment such as tents, food, and other gear can be transported and set up ahead of time if not packed along with the riders.

Or You Might Try a Dude Ranch! "Saddle up . . . ride 'em out!" Call them "dude" ranches, or "guest" ranches, it makes little difference. The atmosphere is still the same—casual, and tinged with the romance of the Old West. This year you might want to spend some time at one of these ranches, and relax, soak up the fresh air, and gaze at spectacular scenery. Mount up and head off on a trail ride breakfast, where you'll enjoy real sourdough pancakes and freshly brewed coffee, warmed by the embers of a glowing campfire. Or take a guided pack trip into high mountain country, and spend a couple of nights sleeping under a blanket of stars. Some guest ranches are open year round. You make your own plans, set your own schedule, and shuffle along as you please. That's the way it is when you play "cowboy" at one of the friendly guest ranches.

Here you can pick your own brand of fun. Want to loaf and take it easy? You can spend lazy hours under the clearest sky and brightest sun you've ever seen. Want to see some wild country? Climb aboard a sure-footed, well-trained western horse and ride to your heart's content, over open plains or lofty skyline mountain trails. You can revel in unspoiled natural beauty which has changed very little from the virgin wilderness viewed by the first pioneers.

Want to fish? Some of America's great trout streams and quiet, secluded lakes are near at hand with hungry trout ready to give you a tussle. Want to join in a roundup and branding? These activities are common on most western working ranches and are a colorful part of the Old West.

Horseback riding is the most popular activity on a western ranch! With a veteran cowhand to guide you, you'll soon feel right at home astride your trail-wise pony.

Oh, That Strawberry Roan! You can spend nights around a campfire, hearing songs and stories of the Old West. There's often a pow-wow, barbecue, or dance for an evening's fun!

Some riders just pack a lunch and ride to a local scenic attraction. Or you can miss a day's ride if you wish to stay in camp to relax, especially if you think a certain part of a trail ride is too rough for you.

Some packaged horseback vacations are commercial ventures operated by local ranchers, dude ranchers, and outfitters, while others are nonprofit. Many are arranged especially for whole families.

The Long and Short of It Trail rides can be short hour or day rides, weekend affairs, or ten-day to two-week jaunts. Generally, most trail ride groups include riders from all walks of life and all 50 states and many other parts of the world, varying in age from youngsters to senior citizens. Among such gatherings you will naturally find some expert riders, but most will be lacking in riding ability. All members are mounted on gentle steeds that prefer to walk (this is basic on mountain trails) at a leisurely pace all day so that the beginning rider has as much fun as the experienced horseman.

Where to Write For information on backpacking trips, guides, and outfitters, write to the appropriate local Chamber of Commerce. For group trips, write to The American Forestry Association, 919 17th Street, N.W., Washington, D. C. 20006, or The Wilderness Society, 729 15th Street, N.W., Washington, D. C. 20005, or The Sierra Club, 1050 Mills Tower, San Francisco, California 95814.

Other Sources You probably can find the names and addresses of trail ride outfits by checking the advertising sections of national outdoor magazines such as *Sports Afield, Outdoor Life, Field & Stream*, and others.

Looking Across the Nation To save time looking in the yellow pages of your telephone book, here are a few other tips:

Arizona

Write to Fred Harvey Company, Grand Canyon National Park, 96023. A mule trip is a fine way to view the Grand Canyon. To avoid the crowds why not visit the Grand Canyon this spring? The weather is delightful, accommodations are easier to obtain, and the scenery magnificent. All the summer facilities are available, too. You can ride Fred Harvey's sure-footed mules down to Phantom Ranch, watch Hopi Indians perform their ceremonial dances, and take trail rides or pack trips into the interior. During the off-season, mule trips down into the mile deep canyon are more available, in contrast to the summer months when they are booked months in advance.

If you are healthy and adventurous, one of the best ways to see the canyon is atop a mule. From this vantage point the "mule skinner" can really appreciate the canyon in its many moods—the plant and animal life, the changing climate, and the story of geological ages told in its walls.

Mules are used rather than horses because of their endurance and patience. It is also said that the mule is very solicitous of its own skin and, therefore, seldom takes chances which would involve its own safety, or that of its rider.

One-day Trip. The one-day Bright Angel Trail trip takes visitors to Plateau Point, on the brink of the inner gorge, high above the raging current of the Colorado River. The trip, which starts at 9 a.m. and ends at 4 p.m., includes guide service and a box lunch for the noon stop. It cover a distance of 12-miles round trip and costs $11.50.

Two-day Trip. The two-day Bright Angel trail trip to Phantom Ranch starts down the Bright Angel Trail at 10 a.m. and goes to Indian Gardens, then over the river trail to follow the inner gorge, crossing the Colorado River over the famous 400 foot suspension bridge, not far from Bright Angel Creek. The price is $35, and includes guide services, meals, and overnight accommodations at Phantom Ranch. The round trip covers 18 miles.

California's High Sierra Vacation

If the most rugged and spectacular is your thing, try the John Muir Trail, part of the famous Pacific Crest Trail System from the Canadian border to Mexico. The John Muir Trail starts in my old Ranger district, at Tuolumne Meadows in Yosemite National Park, and meanders along the western side of the High Sierra Range. The trek to Mt. Whitney along this section is 175 miles long, and passes through the John Muir Wilderness and Yosemite and Sequoia-King Canyon National Parks. In this area, there are some peaks that exceed 14,000 feet, with many over 13,000 feet. Mt. Whitney staggers through the clouds at 14,496 feet!

Packing in Yosemite National Park

Why not try a trail ride or pack outfit safari in world famous Yosemite National Park in the High Sierra Nevada Range? There are exciting trail trips, including a circular route to spectacular country and waterfalls, or a ride out to the largest trees in the world!

Of the 1,189 square miles within the boundaries of Yosemite National Park, more than 1,100 lie in the vast High Sierra region west of the crest of the Sierra Nevada Range.

This is a fabulous stretch of mountains, defying adequate description but possessed of jagged peaks, tumbling streams, friendly meadows dotted with delicate blossoms, deep blue lakes lying in the shadows of glacier-scarred cliffs, and green forests which change in nature as the elevation rises from the cedars, pines, and

Boats on Wallowa Lake look infinitesimal from this vantage point high on the moraine overlooking the lake and Wallowa Mountains. Horsemen find untold recreation in the high Wallowas and Eagle Cap Wilderness Area south of the lake. Both modern accommodations and a state park camping area are available at the lake, accessible by paved Oregon Highway 82, east of La Grade, and Oregon 11 and 204, east of Pendleton. (Oregon State Highway Department photo.)

firs of the lower levels to the wind-twisted hemlocks and white bark pine of the Hudsonian zone (10,000 ft.).

Here the trials of everyday existence seem to melt away and in their place come carefree days and unforgettable nights when the only sounds are the easy sighing of the wind in the tree tops and the peaceful splashing of a brook.

To see all this exciting country at close hand was once difficult, requiring either an arduous back-packing trip or an elaborate (and costly) saddle trip. Now, however, anyone may travel through the most wonderful parts of this primitive vastness in comfort and at a minimum expense.

There are miles of well-marked trails, designated camping and stock grazing areas, and telephone networks. To be sure, some trails are long and strenuous, but by thoughtful planning the whole park can be seen by anyone in good health and of average stamina.

Arranged roughly in a circle are five permanent summer High Sierra Camps. (Tuolumne Meadows is not included among these.) On the average, these are located about nine miles apart, and each of the five is at an area of outstanding beauty and interest. Camps provide accommodations in tents, housing beds with spring and mattress, linen, and ample blankets (nights are cold!). Breakfast and dinner are served in a central dining tent and, though simple, the quality and preparation of the food is excellent and quantities are ample. There are hot showers at each camp, and these are a welcome luxury in the wilderness, especially at the end of a day on the trail. Other essential plumbing is enclosed and of the running water type.

You can also contact the Northern California Horseman's Association for non-profit trail rides held each April, June, and Labor Day weekend.

In November, the Annual Death Valley Trail Riders take off from Indian Wells, and head through two mountain ranges in desert country and end in Death Valley National Monument. Contact Dell Schmitz, Route 1, P.O. Box 3518, Ridgecrest, California 93555.

You can have fun trail riding and packing on the East slope of the Sierra Nevada Range by making reservations with Ray and Judy Holmgren, operators and owners of The Little Antelope Lodge and Pack Station, P.O. Box 105, Coleville, California 96107.

Another famous pack outfit is the DeCarteret Pack Trains, operating in Kings Canyon and Sequoia National Parks and the surrounding National Forest in the High Sierras of California. The address is W. E. DeCarteret, P.O. Box 61, Three Rivers, California 93271.

Colorado

The Colorado unit of the Wilderness Society plans about twelve horseback vacation rides each year. Clifton R. Merritt, Director of Field Services, says "We plan to have not more than 10 or 12 guests on each trip. The treks begin April 1 and the last one of the year goes into the Pecos Wilderness, in mid-September."

Wilderness Society Rides. Wilderness Society rides are timed so that riders may see the most spectacular landscapes on the North American continent at their most beautiful. For example, the trip into the Bob Marshal Wilderness Area is scheduled each year when most of the flowers are at the peak of their blooming season. Trips into Pecos and Gila Wilderness of the Southwest occur in the fall when weather is cool and almost perfect. For full details, write to The Wilderness Society, 5850 E. Jewel Avenue, Denver, Colorado 80222.

No matter how you look at it, from horseback or car, Colorado is a land of contrasting beauty and varied recreation. Riding, fishing, camping, hiking, boating, golfing, or sightseeing await vacationers.

Also in Colorado, the land of big mountains, you will find two Sangre de Cristo Trail rides: one in mid-July, the other in late August. The rides begin at Salida and wind their way to the Great Sand Dunes National Monument. Contact Art Graves, Box 323, Salida, Colorado 81201 to reserve times.

You can get a list of western dude ranches by writing to Colorado Dude & Guest Ranch Association, 210 Clayton Street, Denver, Colorado 80206.

Frontier Air Lines of Denver, Colorado 80202, has 42 selected ranches and packaged riding trips. The six-day Black Hills Trail Ride costs $120 for adults and $90 for children under 16. This includes wrangling, horse feed, all meals, and entertainment.

Idaho

Idaho offers fine riding along the Chief Joseph Trail. This trail winds its way along the path taken by the heroic Nez Perce Indian Chief Joseph during his war with the U. S. Army. For full details, write George B. Hatly, Box 304, Moscow, Idaho 83843.

For summer trail rides, river running, and fall hunting, you might try Bill Guth and Sons who are white water boatmen and licensed outfitters and guides who trek into the heart of Idaho's famous primitive areas. Write to them at Box 705, Salmon, Idaho 83467. You will get the thrill of your life, plus some of the world's best hunting and fishing!

Illinois

A popular trail ride in the mid-west is the 100-mile ride of the Illinois State Stock Horse Association. For dates and other pertinent information, contact Mr. Art Chambers, P.O. Box 159, Havana, Illinois 62644.

Fire Control Officer Theodore W. Paullin and a "short string" in high country in the Bob Marshall Wilderness, Montana. Officer Paullin is a veteran of over thirty years in the Spotted Bear District, which still uses pack strings to transport supplies up to thirty miles a day.

Montana

The Montana State Chamber of Commerce publishes a list of outfitters handling family horseback vacations and lists outfitters that pack hunters into isolated regions. Write to the Chamber of Commerce, Helena, Montana 59601.

The 320 Ranch and the Nine-Quarter Circle Ranch are both located in the famous Gallatin Gateway area. Both ranches offer special rates for families or groups, and they will gladly pick you up at either West Yellowstone or Bozeman if arrangements are made in advance. Both make trips into Yellowstone National Park and Gallatin National Forest. The Nine-Quarter Circle Ranch has a private air strip, and offers pack trips of any duration into the scenic rugged mountain wilderness nearby.

Missouri

The National Scenic Trail Ride in Missouri provides a five day trip for adults at $64.50, with children under 12 at $44.50. If you don't have your own horse, add $7.50 per day for horse rental.

Two fine family horseback vacation rides can be enjoyed in the Ozark Mountains of Missouri. There is a National Scenic Trail Ride with headquarters in Big Springs State Park, and you can obtain details from Mr. Bill Stronsler, 116 W. Main, Houston, Missouri 65483. The other ride is the Cross Country Trail Ride with headquarters in Alley Springs State Park; write to Mr. Ralph Branson, Bland, Missouri 65014. Either of these Ozark trail rides are excellent for beginners since the terrain is not as rugged and steep as in the Rocky Mountain regions. The trail winds around mountains and fords rushing streams containing trout. For the adventurous, there are caves to explore.

New Mexico

If you like rough and rugged country to ride in, New Mexico's Gila Wilderness is an ideal arid primitive region of box canyons surrounded by the 10,000 foot peaks of the Mogollon Mountains. A trail ride across this unspoiled piece of nature's real estate can be done in three days, but a week is recommended. On this trip, you can explore caves and cliff dwellings along the way, discover Indian artifacts, see bear and deer, and fish for scrappy fish in brawling streams. Contact the Forest Supervisor, Attention Information and Educational Division, U. S. Forest Service, Gila National Forest, Silver City, New Mexico 88061.

Pennsylvania

The Flying W Ranch, Kellettville, Pa. 16351, also offers two six-day rides, one during the last week of June when the mountain laurel is in bloom, the other at the end of August. The Flying W also sponsors weekend rides. Another well-recommended vacation is the annual six-day July ride of the Fryburg Saddle Club, Fryburg, Pennsylvania 16326.

South Dakota

One of the better known non-profit organizations is the Black Hills Trail Ride Association, Box 741, Rapid City, South Dakota 57701. The annual ride is held the first week of August. Informality is the key to these adventurous trail rides. Youngsters and adults soon learn to mingle with the other guests, and most of all, each one learns to lend a helping hand without being asked to anyone who may be in need. Some prefer to sleep in sleeping bags out in the open beneath the stars and be lulled to sleep by a murmuring stream, the mournful yipping of a coyote, the hooting of an owl, or the sharp cry of a loon gliding above an alpine lake. Dormitory-type tents are furnished for girls and women who have been traveling alone. The trail ride lasts for six wonderful days. To condition the tenderfoot (or bottomed) riders, an easy, short ride is scheduled for the first day. After that, about 15 to 18 miles will be covered each day with something new standing out around each bend in the trail. All trails are selected and planned so riders can enjoy some of the Black Hills' more outstanding scenery.

The Flying W Dude Ranch, Star Route 2, Tionesta, Pennsylvania.

Evening entertainment, which is typical of many packaged trail rides, means listening to music and legends from wranglers and guides, joining the group around the evening campfire for a songfest (usually off key), and dancing on the hard packed ground.

There are many other organized trail rides, and no two are exactly alike. Some welcome non-riders and furnish transportation over easy trails by wagons. Others feature jazz band concerts, nightly square dances, or hayrack rides on moonlit nights.

Texas

Texas offers some fine opportunities for trail rides. One of the most popular is the Salt Grass Trail Ride, ending at the Houston Stock Show and Rodeo. The ride follows an old frontier days cattle trail route over which thousands of cattle were once driven. It attracts riders from all 50 states and many foreign countries. Recently, over 2,000 riders and 60 wagons made the 90 mile trek. Contact Mrs. Lynne Chesnar, 2332 West Holcome, Houston, Texas 77000.

Wyoming

Wyoming has a new outfitters' directory available. Write to Wyoming Travel Commission, 2320 Capitol Avenue, Cheyenne, Wyoming 82001.

When writing for information regarding how to get there, prices, etc., be sure to request accurate information on what to bring in the way of personal gear.

For trail rides or pack trips, Glidden McNeel and Sons will offer you fabulous scenery with a trail ride or pack safari through the Snake River Range of the Rockies in the Targhee National Forest. Glidden Mc-

Neel is one of Wyoming's top outfitters for big-game hunts, with over 30 years experience.

If You Go by Train If you do not go by bus, private car, or air, you can go by train! North of the border, there are many fine dude ranches along and near the right-of-ways of the Canadian National and Canadian Pacific railways. South of the border, dude and guest ranches dot the countryside east and west along the routes of the Great Northern, Northern Pacific, Union Pacific, Southern Pacific and Sante Fe railroads. For information regarding rail travel to dude ranches, write to the ticket agent concerned or to the chamber of commerce near the area you are interested in. For Canada, write to the Canadian Government Travel Bureau in Ottawa, or to one of the provence travel bureaus listed here:

Newfoundland & Labrador Tourist Development Office, Confederation Building, St. John's, Newfoundland.

Department of Tourist Development, Prince Edward Island Travel Bureau, Charlottetown, Prince Edward Island.

Nova Scotia Travel Bureau, 5670 Spring Garden Road, Halifax, Nova Scotia.

Department of Natural Resources, Travel and Tourist Development Branch, 796 Queen Street (P.O. Box 1030), Fredericton, New Brunswick.

Department of Tourism, Fish and Game, Tourism Branch, 930 St. Foy Road, Québec, Québec.

Department of Tourism & Information, 185 Bloor Street East, Toronto 5, Ontario.

Department of Tourism and Recreation, 408 Norquay Building, 401 York Avenue, Winnipeg 1, Manitoba.

Department of Industry and Commerce, Tourist Development Branch, Power Building, Regina, Saskatchewan.

Alberta Government Travel Bureau, 1629 Centennial Building, Edmonton 15, Alberta.

Department of Travel Industry, Victoria, British Columbia.

Travelarctic, Tourist Development Section, Yellowknife, Northwest Territories.

Department of Travel and Information, P.O. Box 2703, Whitehorse, Yukon Territory.

Outfitters Offer the Best in Outdoor Vacations Where else can you find a family or individual vacation wrapped up for you in such a reasonable package? Members of Associations are carefully screened and inspected before being accepted and their information can be considered reliable. They must follow Fish and Game regulations to comply for licenses to outfit. Each outfitter will offer a different type of service, and his rates will be adjusted accordingly. Some will provide accommodations at the ranch for those who can't take the wilderness vacation. Fish and Game instructions and regulations are generally explained to you by the outfitter.

About Clothes Since dude ranch and outfitter life is, above all, informal, anything goes in the way of clothes. No use carrying heavy baggage both ways, so buy your

Western clothes out here. You can dress authentically Western for ten dollars and up. Typical ranch wear ranges from jeans for both men and women, to saddle pants plus bright shirts, comfortable boots or shoes, and big hats.

About Children Nothing thrives on a ranch like youngsters who are growing up. Bring them, by all means. Most ranchers cater to family parties, and a great many of them have children's playgrounds and counselors.

When Is the Best Time to Come? The dude ranch and outfitter season is traditionally May through October, and the natives will tell you that June, September, and October are the most beautiful months in the West. Most ranches are open from four to six months, but many are open all year, so come when you can get away. There's no closed season on Western hospitality.

Transportation Store your car for the vacation, and come by train, plane, or bus. Any transportation office will be happy to help you plan your trip to the West. Any member ranch will make reservations through a car rental service to have a car waiting for you when you arrive. We suggest that you check with the ranch of your choice for the details of transportation facilities available.

About Your Horse Beginning or experienced riders and children will find mounts well suited to their abilities available. Good horses and the West's dude ranches and outfitters are synonymous.

About Hunting Big game in season, of course. Some individual ranches specialize in hunting parties, so write to the individual ranchers for specific details.

The Big Sky Country The West offers you a vacation to remember, whether you want to relax and listen to the crackle of a campfire after a horseback ride into the wilderness, or fish a fast moving stream where trout put up a real fight, or hunt fossils on the plains, or perhaps bag the big game trophy of the year, or just take a walk in the woods. From the high mountain peaks to the rugged country on the plains, whatever your taste in vacationing, you and your family will be able to find it on a dude ranch or an outfitter pack trip. On some of the operating stock ranches, you can even share the chores with the ranch hands, and you can go as rough as you want or take it as soft as you wish. You can find just about any type of Safari you want!

A backpacking and burro party in the John Muir Wilderness Area. An estimated 60 percent or more of the recreationists backpack into the area. Probably about 15 percent rent burros or a walking mule, and the rest use some combination of commercial or privately owned pack and saddle animals.

5

Start with a Walking and Burro Safari

The Junior Pack Trip The advantage to this is that those who are handicapped or cannot tote even the moderate load required by the backpacker, or those who prefer more comfort than the dyed-in-the-wool go-light knapsacker would consider can still go and enjoy a scenic mountain pack outfit vacation.

Another point in favor of using donkeys is that, with the exception of backpacking, it is the least expensive mode of travel for the budget-minded family that doesn't want to burden themselves packing their camping gear and grub on their own backs. And these friendly beasts of burden cost only $3.50 per day, half as much as a horse or mule. In this manner, the burro (sometimes reluctantly) ambles along carrying the load, led by the unburdened walker. By using a burro more food and comfortable camping equipment can be carried, and one can travel further and stay longer in the beautiful alpine country. Again, the trip can be still further extended if each member of the party will carry a lightweight knapsack with a load of about 25 pounds.

Why Donkeys Are Favored Outdoor organizations have found that the little jackass is the most desirable beast of burden for the beginning packer, and he also remains the favorite pack animal of many experienced campers. In the desert country this little "character" is called by his Spanish name, *El Burro*, and in the highlands of the West, he is called *Mountain Canary*. When the little fellow becomes cantankerous and obstinate he is sometimes called profane names in many languages!

Horses and mules require more care than burros, and must be shod. The little burro has tougher feet and goes barefoot! Thus, a hiker doesn't have to worry about a loose horseshoe or about having to shoe a pack animal far from the home pack station.

Planning the Donkey Safari Much planning and preparation is needed before a burro pack train leaves the corral, just as much as for a horse or mule outfit. The first thing is to decide upon what area you want to visit. What will the starting point be? Check with the Forest or Park officials to see if the area is open to camping and livestock, as some areas are closed due to high fire danger during certain months, and since saddle and pack stock may be required to graze in certain locations. Find out if burros are available near to the takeoff point or have to be trucked in to the end of the road. Not all pack stations have these small packers for rent. Like larger pack animals, burros must be reserved months in advance, since most pack outfits are booked for most of the summer months and all of the hunting season. Nevertheless, the work entailed can be fun and entertaining for the whole family. Maps must be obtained and studied, and routes outlined and decided upon, including whether to back-track and return over the same trail or make a loop trip out of it. If you end the trek somewhere other than the point of departure, the animals must be deadheaded back to the home corral, and you will be charged for this extra service.

Number of "Donks" Needed To answer this question, the pack load must be known. The number of animals you require will depend on three things: the size of your party, the length of the trip, and how much gear you want to take along. Naturally, extra weight means extra animals to pack it, unless you decide to backpack the extras yourself in a knapsack! If you have a youngster or two with you on the safari, it is advisable to take a riding burro along so that the kids can take turns riding when they are tired from hiking. *Don't* put a youngster on top of an already packed burro, as it can overload the burro, unless the animal happens to be lightly packed! Some sort of padding should be placed on top to cushion the rider.

The Load Limit Generally, the weight allowed on a burro may vary from a net load of 50 to 100 pounds. This is due to the difference in ruggedness and steepness of the terrain to be traveled over, and the size, age, and health of the particular animal. A large burro may carry up to 100 pounds; however, station owners generally suggest not over 75 pounds for high country travel.

Amount of Gear You Will Need To determine how much camping gear you will need, it is a good idea to make out a check list. Start by breaking it down into four classifications: food, cooking utensils, sleeping equipment, and duffel. First start with the food items. Plan each meal and make out a menu that is wholesome and satisfactory to all members in the party.

Making Up the Menu In making up the menu for the trip, figure out the number of meals needed on the trip and, for convenience, package each meal in an indi-

Hunters packing their trophy out of the wilderness on a burro.

vidual waxed paper bag, putting breakfast and dinner into a larger plastic bag numbered for the day it is to be used. Lunch material should also be packaged, but should be placed in a top load each day so that it is handy and can be reached easily without having to go through the whole pack load to get it. Avoid wet-pack (canned goods) as much as possible to save on weight. However, add some extra food in case of an emergency layover, or in case you invite some hiker or camper along the trail to share a meal with you. This is also an excellent time to try out some of the new freeze-dried, dehydrated, or concentrated products so that you can choose the kind you will want on the trip. Most of them are very good, and they are lightweight, tasty, and take up less space than other foods. (See list of firms selling these products in the appendix.)

It has been found that a reliable maintenance diet will average out about two and a half pounds of dehydrated or freeze-dried food per person each day. If some canned goods are to be included for special treats, figure total food weight at three pounds per man per day.

Cooking Utensils Cooking utensils and equipment should be light, compact and practical. It is best to purchase one of the two or four man nesting kits and replace the aluminum cups with enamel or plastic cups. Most burro trippers prefer to cook over a camp fire, so you will need a wire grill. Some go-light burro travelers use a small canned gas or gasoline stove. If you cut out the top of a new, square five gallon can it will be useful for carrying water from the stream or lake to camp, handy for heating water, and will fit into a pack box or pannier better than a round one. For dish pans or wash basins, get the plastic kind, as they are lighter and more flexible and will fit in the pack easier. A folding or small Swede bow-saw and a two and a

Burros loaded with outfit and supplies for a trail crew, Flathead National Forest, Montana. (U.S. Forest Service photo.)

half pound single-bit axe are handier than a large heavy axe. An "O" size or Forester shovel will prove useful, and in fact all pack outfits must carry an axe and shovel. Don't forget a pair of pliers, as they always come in handy around camp. Note the check list of equipment suggested.

About Shelter You will need some kind of roof over your head to keep dew or rain off you and your equipment. One or two waterproof tarpaulins are used by the walking packer instead of a tent, because they require no poles, which are hard to pack, and the tarps are more versatile.

The Group Safari In making up your party, select only those friends who you know are congenial and willing to lend a hand with camp chores and burro management. The most experienced camper, woodsman, or mountaineer in the group should be named leader. The leader should be responsible for proper organization and the welfare of the group. He should secure the fire permit required when camping away from improved campgrounds. A meeting of all members going on the trek should be held well in advance of the take-off day. At this time, check lists should be gone over carefully to make sure that proper and sufficient equipment is being gathered. Menus should be made out that are satisfactory to all. Any dietary problem of a member should be discussed and, if necessary, arrangements for special food should be decided on.

Figuring Total Weight Since the approximate pack load must be calculated in advance, the number of pounds of food can be determined by figuring on two and a half pounds of dehydrated and freeze-dried food per day per person, plus a few cans of goodies, for instance, jams, fruit, and tomatoes.

When all food and camping gear is gathered and

Private packhorse family backpacking at Jackson Meadow in the John Muir Wilderness Area. (U.S. Forest Service photo.)

stock-piled, it must be weighed so that the number of pack animals needed can be determined. This information is needed whether you use horses, mules, or burros.

Information the Packer Must Have The packer will need to know well in advance what date you will want to leave, where you plan on going, how many in your party, how long you plan on being away on the trip, and the date you expect to return back to the pack station. He will also need to know the approximate total weight of your outfit. A deposit must be sent in advance of take-off day. If you must cancel the trip, you lose the deposit.

How to Contact a Pack Station Concession Write to the Park Superintendent or Forest Supervisor of the area you are interested in traveling and ask for a list of pack stations that rent burros and other pack stock. You may have to settle for a pack mule if there are no donkeys in the area you want to hike and pack into. You can also write to the State Chamber of Commerce for this information. The addresses of all National Parks and National Forests and their Regional Offices are listed later on in this book.

Burro Gear Before you leave the pack corral, have the outfitter check you out on the handling, care, and feeding of your donkeys. The packer will furnish all tack: saddle blankets, harness, halter, manty or canvas pack cover, pack rope, picket pin and rope, hobbles (if needed), etc. Take a grazing bell or two along so that you will be able to find the animals each morning. Good clean blankets are a must. Don't accept dirt-grimed blankets or blankets with holes in them. Ask the outfitter to throw in a currying brush so that you can keep the animal's back brushed clean. A double-rigged pack saddle is best for steep country. The front cinch on the double-rigged saddle should be pulled tight, but not so snug that you can't get at least two fingers between the cinch and the burro's body. The front cinch should be about three inches in back of the front shoulder so that the flesh will not be pinched and cause a hard-to-heal cinch sore. The rear cinch hangs more loosely so that the animal can breathe freely.

Special Use Permits Outfitters and packers are required to have a Special Use Permit when operating in a National Forest or National Park. The operator must be bonded and must observe all game and forest regulations.

No guide or packer is required when you pack out with burros, but an experienced packer must go with each group when using larger pack animals. Operators have such a short season and too much invested in their stock to let inexperienced people use them. They have found through bitter experience that many of their saddle and pack animals are returned lame, galled, sore-backed, and half starved at times because the renter did not know how to handle or care for stock in the back-country. In some cases, the stock returned to the station corral days ahead of the stranded campers.

Do It Yourself Packers You can learn to pack! Read up on the subject first, gain book knowledge, and then go out into the field and practice. Go to the nearest pack station and have the station personnel teach you to pack and balance a pair of kyacks and sling them on a sawbuck pack saddle, and how to throw a simple pack hitch.

Recommended Reading *All About Camping*, by W. K. Merrill, $3.95, The Stackpole Company, Kelker & Cameron Streets, Harrisburg, Pa. 17105; *Going Light With Backpack and Burro*, Sierra Club, $2.50, The Sierra Club, 1050 Mills Tower, San Francisco, California 94104, and *Joe Back's Famous Horses, Hitches, and Rocky Trails*, $2.75, Sage Books, Chicago, Illinois.

6

The Technique of Burro Handling

Burro Management The science of burro management lies in getting these sometimes balky and reluctant beasts to do what one wants them to do. These little pack animals can be very obstinate at times! You just have to be smart enough to outmaneuver them. Generally, burros are more responsive than mules and are quick to respond to gentleness along with a little coaxing.

What Causes Stubbornness Stubbornness may be an attempt by the burro to see what he can get away with. When he realizes that he can't get by with anything, he will soon settle down and be his regular friendly self.

My personal experience over the years with burros is that they are more stubborn than mules, but like their big cousins, there is usually a reason for this. Generally, this has been caused by the animal being mishandled and abused by former owners, or from inexperienced burro-trippers overloading the animal, and not giving him enough time to drink his fill or to graze. You can't blame the burro for any physical handicap either. He

A burro unwillingly transporting supplies in Lincoln National Forest, New Mexico. Even well-trained donkeys can be stubborn at times. (U.S. Forest Service photo.)

may have an old injury that bothers him, he may be too young or too old for an arduous mountain safari, or he may be just tired and worn out from being packed all summer without enough rest at the home corral.

Refusing the Animal When the animal cannot be refused at the pack station because it is the only one left or for other reasons, you will either have to abort the trip or take the beast and make the best of it by packing him lighter and taking it more slowly.

If he is stubborn while climbing a steep trail leading up to a mountain pass at high elevation, he may need to rest for a longer period than usual. If he is obstinate when descending the down trail, he may have stiff shoulders. If he is stubborn on the level, he may be overloaded or perhaps his pack needs to be readjusted; something is hurting him, you may be sure. In a dangerous situation, it may be just plain fear! Perhaps the animal is just showing good judgment not wanting to travel over a dangerous slide area or boggy spot that his master is trying to force him to take.

Learning the Hard Way Years ago, while I was packing mail and supplies into one of my trail crew camps on the San Bernardino National Forest with two burros I had borrowed from a friend, I ran into a balky situation. Several miles out from the Mill Creek Ranger Station, I came to a wet spot in the trail caused by a leaking drainpipe from a nearby spring which ran beneath the trail. I was unable to get either burro to pass the spot. Evidently, the water gurgling underground spooked them. After trying everything but mayhem, I gave it a last try, made the mistake of attempting to push and heave from the rear, and promptly received a vicious kick in the midriff that left a half-inch gash in my belt buckle. I finally won out by turning them around and skirting the spot by back tracking several hundred yards until I found an area where I could climb up the bank through the brush and down again beyond the *no pass* spot. This solved the problem, and I learned a little about burros. I later heard that the trail crew killed several rattlesnakes near the spring. So this was really a *no pass* spot so far as the burros were concerned!

Happy Burros! Normally, with gentleness and kindness, a stubborn donkey can be won over in a few days or a week and become the friendly little rascal he is. Don't forget to bring some cube sugar for burro treats!

Don't Trust Your Stock! Don't trust any pack animal while you are packing. Tie him to a stout tree or post near the pack loads. Some first-time packers learn the hard way when they believe that a pet burro, horse, or mule will stand still all the time while you cinch down on the saddle and start throwing the kyacks on. Sometimes for reasons of his own he will not cooperate, and will take off and buck the whole load off down the side of the mountain. The lead rope should not be fastened less than waist high and the rope should be tied short: just short enough so that he can't get a foot over it and foul the works up. Tying the animal in this manner will discourage him from walking around and around the tree or hitchpost as you attempt to blanket him after he has been groomed.

Grooming the Burro Let us start with a typical day. First comes going over the animal's back with a currycomb or brush. I pack a good stiff curry brush as it is much more gentle on a sensitive back. If you are too rough in grooming, you will soon learn which end kicks and which end bites! The main object is to keep the animal as clean and neat as possible. Don't forget to brush his legs free of caked mud and debris, but be careful! While the kick of a burro is not as damaging as that of a horse or mule, it can cause painful injuries.

Watch the burro's ears, and if they are laid back along his neck—watch out! When grooming or packing a burro, stand in a position that will make it difficult for him to bite or kick.

Dressing the Burro Experienced packers hardly ever have to treat sore backs—they prevent them! Clean backs covered with soft smooth pads or blankets, properly fitted saddle and harness with well balanced loads, all properly lashed down with one of the pack-hitches will prevent galls and sore backs.

If for any reason a saddle or cinch sore does occur, every effort should be taken to avoid further irritation. The harness and blanket pads may need adjustment, the load may need to be lightened, or the whole load pulled and redistributed among the sound burros. Most experienced packers carry some brand of veterinarian approved salve, cream, or healing powder, while others make up their own healing concoctions. (See the chapter on *First Aid for Your Mount.*)

Saddling Up! After the burro's back has been brushed clean and the saddle sweat-pad (corona) and top blanket have been inspected to check that both are free of debris, such as pine needles, dirt, burrs, small twigs, or anything abrasive, you can saddle up.

The Nigh Side Always work from the "nigh" (left) side. Place the sweat pad evenly on the burro's back close to his neck, and then slide the pad backward so that it extends about three inches beyond where the front edge of the saddle will be. This action tends to smoothe the hair backwards into its natural direction, and will keep it from bunching up and causing a hot spot. The wool saddle blanket goes next, on top of the sweat pad.

Next comes the sawbuck saddle. Lay the cinch and latigo across the top of the saddle and place the saddle

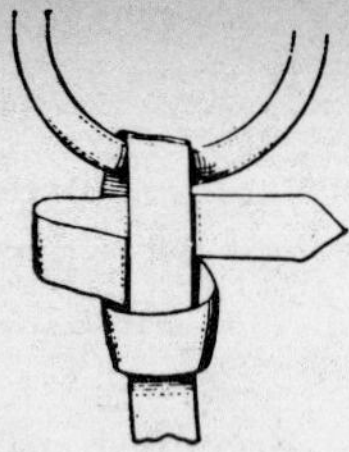

Overhand.

Double half hitch.

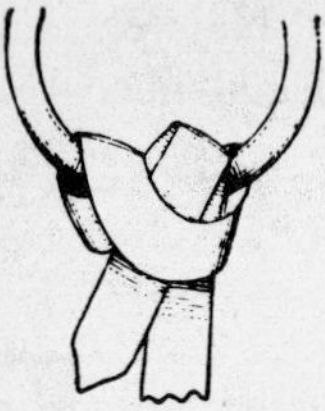

Clove.

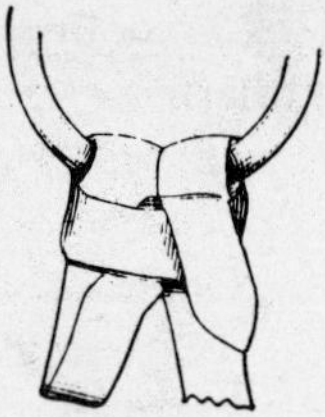

Double half hitch with draw loop.

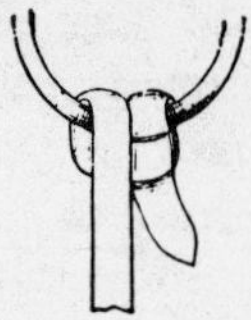

Modification of double half hitch.

Latigo ties.

on the animal's back, not too close to the neck so that the ends of the saddle won't dig into his withers. The front of the sawbuck fits into the hollow just behind the withers. Drop the cinch gently over the off-side and reach under the animal, pick it up and cinch the saddle down with the latigo. (Note latigo ties in the illustrations.)

The forward cinch can hardly be too tight. Nevertheless, you should be able to get at least two or three fingers between it and the animal's chest. If the cinch is too tight, you will probably cause a cinch welt. The second cinch (in the rear of a double-rigged pack saddle) should be loose enough so that it does not impede the animal's breathing.

The Breeching Next, bring the breast strap around and fasten to the saddle. Here comes the tricky-sticky

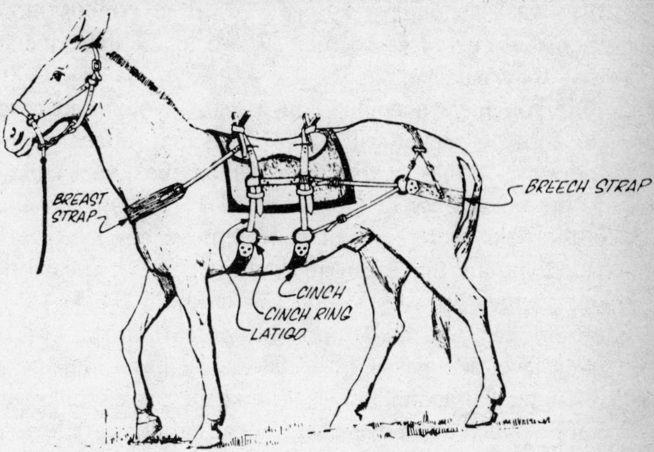

Pack animal saddled and ready to pack.

side of putting the harness on! Gently slide the breeching back over the burro's rear-end, always remembering that this is the kicking end! Reach out as far as you can from the side and slip the burro's tail over the back of the breeching. Some animals are sensitive around their tails, and if you are unable to get the animal's cooperation in this maneuver, leave his tail alone. Later on, as the animal warms up along the trail, you might be able to free it so that the burro can swat flies with his built-in swatter.

Packing the Burros Can Be Fun! The weight a burro can carry has been discussed earlier. The important factor is not to overload him, and to have the kyacks or panniers evenly matched and balanced. I carry a spring scale with a 60 pound weight pull. By using the scale I am able to keep my loads balanced. If one of the kyacks should weigh two or three pounds more than the other, I add a rock or two to the light one so that they balance.

If you have a companion assisting you in loading, the off side packer will lift his load first, attaching the loops or leather "ears" from which the kyacks hang to the cross trees of the sawbuck. The reason for this is that it is more convenient to remove this kyack last when you are unpacking the outfit alone. The near-side packer then attaches his load. When both kyacks loops are hooked, and the straps adjusted so that the kyacks hang level and parallel, the packs are lifted and eased down on the animal's sides so that the pack saddle will not be pulled off to one side. Canvas panniers are loaded so that the off side unit of the pair is provided with a strap which is brought over the top center of the sawbuck and secured tightly to the near side pannier. This has a tendency to pull both kyacks or panniers slightly away from the sides of the animal. Next, stand behind the pack animal to check if the load is balanced. If the saddle is resting straight, but one of the kyacks is lower than the other, correction can be made by adjusting the "ear" loop buckle. If the loops are non-adjustable, rematch all kyacks in the pack string to obtain suitable balance.

The Top Load Bulky or light gear such as a tent or sleeping bags, catch-feed, etc., goes on as a top load. Compact bedding rolls and dunnage bags are fine. A single bedroll goes crosswise between the cross trees of the saddle. Two sleeping bags in canvas duffel bags go lengthwise, one resting on top of each kyack or pannier. Inspect the load from the rear looking forward. If the whole load looks right, carefully spread a canvas manty or canvas pack cover over the load. If the canvas is too large, pull it off and fold it to a size that will

An example of a neat packing job.

come down to the bottom edge of the kyacks on either side.

Taking Off At Last! When there are several campers in the party, it is advisable to lead each animal during the first day or two and on the last day when heading for the home corral. Whenever the going gets rough, all burros should be led. After being out on the trail for several days, the animals are sometimes allowed to travel free when circumstances permit. However, check with Forest or Park regulations in this regard. In some areas stock is not allowed to trail free, especially when nearing places of habitation or on trails heavily traveled by foot and pack trains. When the animals are trailing free, the tie or lead rope should be secured to the ring provided for that purpose on most pack saddles, or if there is no ring, it should be tied to the top of the pack with just enough rope so that the animal can reach water when crossing a stream, yet not become entangled.

Passing Pack Strings and Riders On hearing or sighting riders or a pack string approaching, lead your burros off the trail to one side so that the larger and faster animals may pass.

The Pace—Miles per Day When traveling with burro, one might just as well reconcile himself to a slow pace. There is no use in fretting, because a speed of about 1½ to 2 miles per hour is about par for the trail! This pace is just about right when traveling with a family group, especially if there are children along. Burros just cannot be hurried, and as long as they keep moving, there is little you can do about it. Nevertheless, at times the string will slow down to an unreasonable gait —even for jackasses. The animal knows that he can see the person leading him and can tug against the rope, especially if being led. However, he is apprehensive of anyone walking behind him, especially if that person carries a willow switch. If you have an extra slow burro in the lead, drop him to the end of the string, and he will generally try to keep up with the rest. *Don't* make the mistake of shouting, or threatening the burros continually. This makes them spooky and more obstinate.

Try and keep the pack train moving. If a short rest period is necessary when negotiating a steep stretch of trail, or for time out for a child, hold the animals so that they will not bunch up or mill about, otherwise some will start off the trail to graze, lie down, or wander off. You can't blame the animals if they want to lie down, since it is uncomfortable supporting a pack when standing idle. I have had certain members of a string sit down, lie down, and even roll—requiring repacking the load on that particular burro.

About eight to ten miles of travel per day is about right. If you get off in the morning around 9 a.m. and make camp around 3:30 or 4 p.m. you will have time to make a comfortable camp, stake out or turn loose the pack string, have a hearty camp meal, and finish the chores before dark. Some families leave early and make camp by noon so that the kids can have a nap-rest and not become too tired to enjoy the trek.

Trail Grazing Grazing along the trail should not be permitted, unless the animals have learned to snatch a bite here and there without stopping. *Do not* permit the pack animals to run! They can get out of control, and besides, it takes a really tight pack hitch to hold the load together under this treatment. Any loose kettles or other noisy objects that will rattle inside the kyacks can spook the less excitable animals if a bad actor in the string cuts up and wants to run. While burros don't buck as hard as a horse or mule, they can kick up their heels and shake up the contents of the pack load, making a witches brew of anything that isn't well wrapped or can break loose inside: mixing flour, sugar, coffee, etc., into a mess that is unusable.

Every member of the party should be alert and constantly watch to see if any of the animals appear to be distressed. When something is wrong, the burro will sometimes edge off the trail, stop, sit down or attempt to roll. That generally is a sign that something is radically wrong, so stop the pack train and investigate at once. It usually means throwing the whole pack until the difficulty is found. As you walk along, check all animals, and look to see if any of the packs have shifted. Has the blanket slipped? Is the cinch too tight or too loose? If you do not check these things as you travel along, you are going to have some sorebacked burros if anything has gone wrong and you didn't catch it in time! You will also have some explaining to do to the pack station owner who rented you the animals. If a sorebacked burro is brought in from a trip, it may mean weeks of healing before the animal can be packed again, costing his owners many weeks of lost rental.

The Mid-Day Siesta Knock off at least for an hour and give both man and beast a rest. If at all possible, the animals should be tied in the shade in a level spot, far enough apart so that they will not quarrel and interfere with each other. Burros are individualists and like their separate spheres of influence. As I mentioned before, tie the lead rope high and short enough. Now remove the pack rope, lift the top pack load off, and then remove the kyacks and dunnage out of the animal's reach. Spread the manty (canvas cover) over the packs to protect the contents from the weather. Next, loosen the cinches on all animals, but do not release them, otherwise the saddles may slip under the burro's bellies and cause a riot. Leaving the saddles on will speed repacking after lunch. Personally, I throw the whole works so that I can check for sore backs, and also to give their backs a chance to cool. It only takes a few minutes to repack and head along the trail.

Watch Out for Swampy Spots and Snow in Passes! Burros fear swampy spots and tracking through soft snow in high mountain passes. Their small hooves do not give them much support under a load. One may encounter these conditions in the early part of the season and at times may have an animal bog-down to his belly or on his side. Avoid these spots if possible by going around them, or back track and see if you can go around above or below them.

If You Do Get Bogged Down! When an animal becomes mired, his struggles cause him to sink deeper and his legs may disappear as he rests on his belly or side. He will be shaking with fear, snorting, and struggling for solid bottom. Approach him slowly and keep talking to him quietly to calm his fears. Remove the pack, saddle, and all gear. Cut the ropes if necessary. If he is unable to extract himself, you will have to assist him in getting out of the difficulty. You might have one member of the party pull on his lead rope while another lifts up on his tail. One time my pet burro got so mired that nothing seemed to work. Finally I made a large loop with the pack rope, placing the loop around the animal over its rump, and passing the running end through the halter-ring. With three of us pulling, the struggling burro managed to reach firm ground. It was half an hour before the brave little fellow became calm and collected enough to repack. After he dried off, it was quite a job cleaning the caked mud off his underside and legs.

In addition to boggy terrain, burros dislike soft snow. However, they can cross over snow patches found in high mountain passes as late as July if they do not sink over their hooves. Where snow blocks the passes, any holes should be filled in and packed down. Sometimes it is necessary for members of a burro safari to break trail through the soft stretches by walking back and forth until the snow in the trail path is packed solidly enough for the burros to walk over. Sometimes the packs may have to be thrown, and each individual animal led across. The burros should be *led* over or around any dangerous spots, and not left to cross on their own. Fortunately, it is possible at times to skirt snow patches that the burro has objections to.

Like mules, burros are surefooted, and can travel over any stretch of rough trail which they will undertake willingly. In exceptionally rough spots, assistance over obstacles may be given by having members of the party lift up on the pack, one on each side. Caution must be taken by the helper on the bank side to avoid being crushed between kyack and unyielding rocks, and by the helper on the nigh-side to keep from being pushed over the trail edge as the burro struggles past the tight spot.

Fording Mountain Streams Because of their small hooves, burros dislike crossings with soft sand or mud, so, if possible, cross on gravel beds, preferably at a point where the water is quiet so that the bottom can be observed. Generally, burros can ford any stream a person can wade without swimming. Don't attempt a crossing where the water is swift and deep enough to reach the bellies of these little animals. Some burros will cross swift shallow streams without a pause while others may require considerable urging.

Picking the Right Campsite If you have planned properly, you will have found out in advance where and how far apart good camping spots will be along the trail route you are traveling.

The hunters at this camp in the Mt. Baker National Forest, Bellingham, Washington, have chosen a beautiful campsite. They are taking advantage of the special early "High Mountain Buck Deer Season" held in September, which permits hunting in high alpine areas before they are snowed in and inaccessible. (U.S. Forest Service photo by Robert J. DeWitz.)

The requisites for a good campsite are safety, nearness to firewood, a supply of pure water for both man and beast, and sufficient forage for the pack animals. Here are some tips that should be helpful in camp selection:

Never camp under large tall trees which may act as lightning rods, or near dead snags where wind or the elements may cause limbs or trees to fall on you or your camp. These are called "widow makers" by mountaineers.

It is not advisable to make camp in tall dry grass or near heavy brush fields or swamps, for there is a fire hazard ever present in the former, and there are black flies, mosquitos, and gnats that hold forth in heavy brush, and midges or "no-see-ums" near water. However, most insect pests more or less disappear after the middle of July or August.

In the lower elevations, it is needless to say, keep your camp away from poison oak, ivy, and sumac.

Never take it for granted that wilderness water is pure. Boil or treat it chemically to purify it. There may be a winter killed dead animal in the stream above your camp!

If possible, it is best to pitch your tent or tarpaulin fly on higher ground away from an alpine lake or stream edge, and out of the way of high winds, but so that some breeze will keep insects away.

If you use a tent, it should be pitched to take advantage of favorable exposures. Face it toward the southeast to get the morning sun, but place it so that you get some shade in the afternoon.

The tent should, if possible, be pitched on a level knoll or a slight slope so that the ground will drain away from the front. Try to keep away from marshy or clay soils where mud puddles and rain collect.

Be sure that all stones, sharp sticks, and other hard objects are removed from the spot where you want to pitch your tent. Sharp objects can puncture your tent floor and air mattress too!

Keep the prevailing breeze in mind so smoke and sparks from your campfire won't be uncomfortable or burn holes in your canvas gear. Remember that drafts are uphill in the daytime and downhill at night.

If you camp in a canyon, be sure that you pitch your canvas home high enough above any streambed so that you will not get caught in a thunderstorm flash flood. Camping in high mountain canyons can at times be very cold.

Unpacking the Burros When you trail into your chosen campsite in the afternoon, the layout of the camp should be determined as quickly as possible so that the heavy loads may be removed from the animals' backs. Unpack the gear close to where your tent and fire will be, and immediately after the kyacks are lifted off, take the animals to where they will be picketed or turned loose so that the campsite isn't messed up and won't attract flies.

Burro Tack The important thing is to stack all tie ropes, pack harness, and other equipment in one spot. Pack ropes should be coiled, pack covers (mantys) folded, saddles placed on a nearby log or rock, and the saddle blankets laid on top with the animal side up so that they will dry. The kyacks should be lined up in pairs near where the camp fire will be so that everything will be handy for the person who will be the cook.

Fitted Equipment Pack harness and kyacks are fitted to each individual animal, so they should go back on the same animal when they are to be repacked. The pack station operator generally has numbered the panniers and harness so that you will know which outfit goes on each animal. If rain threatens, the saddles and kyacks and other gear may be stacked and the pile protected with a pack canvas. Lead ropes should be collected and hung in one place so that they are not misplaced or lost when you wrangle the burros in the morning.

When you have all helped set up camp and have taken care of the pack stock, assign each member of your party some specific camp chore—and don't forget to have someone dig a latrine at least 50 to 100 yards away from your camp and your water supply. After each use, the pit should be partly covered with dirt. When you break camp, be sure that the pit is completely filled!

Should You Picket, Hobble, or Just Turn Loose? If the burros are not accustomed to being hobbled, they should be belled and turned loose. In some areas, picketing is prohibited because of the damage to alpine meadows. If picketing is allowed, the animals should be staked out in a clear area large enough in circumference so that the picket rope will not get tangled in brush or rocks, thus limiting grazing. Too many burro-trippers fail to move their animals often enough to fresh forage spots, and the burros do not get enough food to enable them to keep their strength for the long haul of the trip. If the animals are not moved every two hours or so, the grass will be eaten down to the roots and the meadow tramped down in bad looking circles. This shows a lack of good burromanship, and the Rangers will certainly call it to your attention!

The One Burro Outfit A single burro is more prone to roam than burros in a group. In this case, it might be wise to picket the animal, at least for the first night or so and the last night out, to keep within bounds any homesickness and urge to head for the home corral and the easy life. If there is more than one burro the whole group will get this urge at times and it is best to keep the animals above your camp. They usually seem to head up canyon to get high enough for the first morning sun.

Burro Groups Since burros stay together if they are picketed, only half the animals generally need to be picketed. Be sure that the animals are separated far enough apart so that each burro has his own grazing circle—otherwise a kicking, biting fight may ensue!

The Stake-out If the outfitter didn't furnish a metal picket-pin, you will have to cut a stake. In any event, cut and drive a good strong stake, as it will be called upon to take considerable strain, and a piece of dead limb generally will not hold. Saplings which are strong enough seldom are close enough and trimming would be required, so it is best to cut a stake. However, do it in a thicket where the damage to the surrounding areas will not be so obvious. There are regulations regarding the cutting of green trees!

Generally, the pack rope is used for a tether-rope. The grazing rope should be tied to the stake at ground level with a clove hitch. Other types of knots are apt to be pulled off the top of the stake. To prevent the animal from winding the knot to the end of the rope and thus being released, it is desirable to tie two half hitches around the running end (long end) with the standing rope (short end). This is a good way to finish off a clove hitch.

If the pack rope isn't long enough, the pack rope of an animal that isn't staked out can be added to increase grazing radius, provided that the added rope will not become entangled with any ground debris. The ropes should be connected with a sheet bend.

Cold Nights Animals walk up and down during the night to keep warm, and in this manner may completely unwind a twisted rope if no swivel is provided. On extra cold nights, protect your stock by using a saddle blanket held in place by a loosely held cinched saddle.

Loose Grazing When burros are turned loose for the night, the grazing bells should go on the more influential animals (leaders). Bell straps should be tight enough so that they remain under the chin, where they are less apt to constrict the windpipe. Unless halters are snug, they should be removed. Animals are apt to step through loose halters at times while grazing and get into a real tangle.

Canyons When camped in canyons, pack stock is invariably turned loose upstream. Most grazing animals seem to prefer this direction, because feed tends to be more lush in the more open upper reaches of high country watersheds. Most burro-trippers like this because the walls of the canyon and the pass beyond form a natural barrier within which to seek the burros in the morning. The stock will generally leave the flat canyon floor but will not usually cross over a pass unless the animals happen to get chummy with a passing pack train. If you happen to make a late start in the morning or plan to lay over for a day or so beware of trail riders and pack strings passing your camp. Burros are rarely guilty of following, but sometimes single horses and mules are prone to be followers.

Drift Fences Both the National Park Service and the Forest Service have constructed drift fences across many mountain canyons. Trail riders and backpackers alike must cooperate in keeping drift fence gates closed. In some backcountry areas, these Services have fenced in meadows where stock may be turned loose, usually with a time limit of 24 hours. The stock must then be removed so that all the forage isn't used up by one party.

Beware of Camp Robbers! There are many of these little woods creatures that will visit your camp during the day or night, especially when you are off hiking and enjoying the scenery. During the day, camp robbing "jays" will steal what they can off your stove or camp table, and deer love to move in while you are off fishing and lick up anything salty in and around camp. Don't forget your pack burros, since these little devils like to stick close to camp and can generally wreck things while foraging for Quaker Oats, salt, sugar, and other goodies in your tent or in the kyacks that you forgot to swing high on a limber limb.

At Night! At night, meadow mice enjoy nibbling the contents of your food packages after they have chewed holes in them, and the little woods "pig" will chew on sweaty clothing, pack harness, and axe handles. Sometimes a friendly bear will pay you a night visit and eat you out of your canvas home away from home. Another favorite bear trick is to come in one way and to go out another way, possibly through the side of your tent, leaving a hole a mule could walk through. I know. It has happened to me! To add insult to injury, the bear will scatter your pack stock over the hill into the next county. Nevertheless, you can discourage the bear by heaving pans and rocks at him if he visits you at night. However, don't throw anything at sounds where you can't see the cause, it might be a skunk! If you ever make this mistake, I can assure you that you will regret it!

Check Burros Before Turning In If you picketed the burros when you made camp, they generally will have eaten nearly all the good forage in a circle by dark, so it is a good idea to move them to another good grazing spot before you turn in for the night, so that they can get their little bellies filled and can start feeding again at daylight.

If an animal has pulled his picket-pin during the night for any reason, he will not go far dragging a picket-rope and will normally stay near his burro friends. If the burros were turned loose during the night and not hobbled, they could be some distance away. In looking for them, you probably will not find them in any nearby lush meadow, because, like horses and mules, they prefer bunch-grass which grows on benches higher up. When turning stock loose, it is best to do so above your camp for a day or so at the beginning, so that you are between the critters and the home corral until they have forgotten about the hay and grain there. Another good spot to look for stray burros is on sunny slopes, where they will stand quietly until they are warmed by the morning sun, at which time they will continue their grazing.

The Bell and Braying Greeting! If you cannot hear a grazing bell, you might be lucky and be able to track your burros, at least up or down the trail or up to a bench. However, it is always a joy to hear the grazing bells near camp and the burros' noisy morning greeting of a serenade begging for a feed of grain or camp scraps. Any leftover biscuits or pancakes from breakfast will do the trick. If the burros were picketed last night and none have broken away you know where they are, and it is no problem to gather them and lead them into camp.

Using Catch Grain Burros (and other stock) are readily caught if you approach slowly while chirping or whistling softly—with an outstretched hand holding an offering of grain. (You did bring catch oats with you, I hope!) They usually are frisky in the morning, so approach slowly, and then quickly snap your tie rope to the lead-ring in their halter and lead them back to camp. If the stock was turned loose without halters, be *sure* to tie the lead rope with a snug bowline knot so that the animal will not be choked or have the loop slide over his head. Never tie any rope around an animal's neck with anything but a bowline knot, as otherwise the animal will strangle to death if the rope pulls tight for any reason! If you have more than two or three burros, it may be preferable to herd-drive them. They will be easier to catch upon arrival at camp if they are not unduly excited. Members of your party left in camp should spread out across the trail when they hear the wrangler(s) coming so that the animals will not go on past camp. Catch the gentle ones first, and then advance on the recalcitrant and suspicious beasts. Pretend that you don't care whether you catch them or not. Look off to one side, and hold out a handful of oats. When you get close enough slip your arm around the animal's neck, have a helper come up slowly with a lead rope. If the animal rears up and bolts, do not chase him, but start the process all over again. If this doesn't work, saddle the rest of the animals, and the ornery member generally will come to heel. Personally, I like to leave the halters on my rented burros. There is not much danger of their catching a hind foot in a halter since they are not shod. Horses and mules will sometimes catch the heel of a hind shoe in a halter when scratching an itch on their heads and will get into real trouble when the shoe heel hooks solidly and throws them.

A hunting camp pitched among the aspens high in the Sangre de Cristo Mountains of northern New Mexico forms a picturesque scene. Notice how each horse is picketed separately and with plenty of grazing room. (Photo courtesy of the New Mexico State Tourist Bureau.)

7

Saddle and Packhorse Hunting Can Be Thrilling!

Wilderness Hunting The traditional use of the National Forests, especially in their Primitive and Wilderness Areas, as public hunting grounds has never diminished. These forests, lands, and waters are the home of uncounted millions of game animals and birds both large and small. Present populations are estimated to amount to more than one-half of all big-game animals in the United States. The State Game Refuges in the National Forests and most of the National Parks that are surrounded by National Forests are protected sanctuaries, and the overflow of game animals from these areas into the forests tends to help provide a continual supply of game animals for the hunter. Pronghorn antelope, mountain goat, bighorn sheep, whitetail, Columbia blacktail and mule deer, elk, moose, black bear, grizzly and Alaska brown bear, mountain lion, and wild boar are among the species hunted each year. Smaller animals such as fox, wolf, raccoon, opossum, rabbit, and squirrel are prime recreational attractions for the camera hunter. Upland birds such as grouse, quail, and turkey are the objects of many hunting safaris. Migratory waterfowl are found on some of the strategically located National Forests lands.

Generally, big-game is the objective of most National Forest hunters. State laws are usually effective in developing and maintaining thrifty game populations. The harvest by hunters should be markedly increased in some regions to prevent decimation of oversized herds through starvation and malnutrition. After a long steady increase, the population of big-game animals in the National Forests and the number harvested annually appear to have stabilized since the last estimate.

Fresh Tracks! The fresh tracks of a black bear or grizzly along a mountain trail, or the hoof print of a deer, moose, or caribou at a lake's edge—a moment like this can strike the centuries from man and starts the red blood surging. You are a hunter again! So enjoy it to the fullest!

Why Backpack When You Can Ride? With a saddle and pack string outfit, you can travel with more comfort, go farther, and stay longer than the hike-in hunter who has to pack all his gear in on his back and must carry out any game killed. This means only a short stay in the woods. It also means that any game collected will require several packboard trips back and forth to the area of the kill to pack the meat out to where it can be transported to the home freezer.

Any "dude" who has ever taken a pack trip will recall it as one of the most thrilling adventures of a lifetime. To most hunters, a successful hunting trek into mountain wilderness is tops, since even if they do not connect with game, they have had a superb experience and have been able to enjoy the majestic scenery. Most hunters with whom I have talked in the field while on game patrol or in town at the local clubs or lodges agree that this is true. There is always a sense of pioneering and exploring in a venture of this sort. The far-off tinkle of grazing bells, the tall tales told around the evening campfire, the trophy head and meat packed over Hell-For-Sure Pass, or the bear that spooked the stock during the night will be long remembered!

It has been my experience that almost all unspoiled wilderness is at least two or three days' ride from a railroad, airport, or road end. The bonus of packhorse hunting is in getting away from the competition of the heavily hunted areas and in greater freedom and chances of connecting with game. The party can wander at will and range well beyond the road end for a week or weeks on end.

How to Get Started A hunting safari with a professional outfitter is ordinarily the best way to get started for the hunter who isn't accustomed to handling, shoeing, and caring for saddle and pack stock and all their complex gear and equipment. Besides, the packer or guide knows where the hunting is at its best. It's his livelihood to have satisfied clients, many of whom come back year after year. Inexperienced horsemen who try to set up their own pack trips with borrowed or untrained stock and equipment collected from friends or rented from a rancher are certain to run into all sorts of difficulties. The pack string is very likely to head back for the home corral when turned out to graze, leaving the would-be packers afoot far back in the woods!

Handling Pack Stock The outfitter and his employees (horse wranglers, cooks, etc.) will do most of the stock management on a pack trip. The client can be of help by staying out of the way, or by following instructions of the packer if he wishes to learn the game. Most hunters offer to do so at some stage of the trek. Many clients and their outfitters and guides become very good friends. The packer generally is willing to show you the tricks of the trade—how to water, feed, hobble, turn loose to graze, bridle, saddle and pack, and even to throw one or more of the pack hitches. All these angles are interesting to most sportsmen. At some future date, if you acquire your own stock, you will know how to care for them on your own mountain safari.

Your Assigned Horse or Riding Mule No responsible outfitter will put a client on anything but a gentle animal. Naturally, it is easier for the whole party when all members of a pack-trip know how to take care of the animals assigned to them. A little coaching from an experienced packer will enable the tenderfoot to help a great deal with the big job of saddling, loading, and cinching down the pack with a Diamond or other pack-hitch. Besides, it can be fun!

The Denali Hunting and Guide Service The National Rifle Association is now registering guides, and sets standards under the Denali program in the form of a directory of qualified and approved hunting guides, outfitters, and hunting camp operators in North America. This program has been established under the Hunting and Conservation Section, Office of the Secretary, National Rifle Association, 1600 Rhode Island Avenue, N.W., Washington, D. C. 20036. The directory may be obtained for $1.

NRA Hunting Code Ethics In signing a contract with a client under this program, hunting service personnel subscribe to a tenpoint "Code of Ethics for Guides, Outfitters, and Hunting Camp Operators." The Code is intended to protect hunters, guides, outfitters, hunting camp operators, and the general public.

Picking a Packer or Outfitter When possible, get a first-hand report on an outfitter from some responsible

Hunter pack string on a trail above Maude Lake near the Great Divide, Selway-Bitterroot Wilderness Area, Clearwater National Forest, Idaho. (U.S. Forest Service photo.)

agency or through the hunting guide service before signing up and paying an advance on reservations. Like any other business, outfits have their share of incompetents. Generally, cut rate outfits are haywire outfits that cut corners and are carelessly managed with poor equipment and halfbroken saddle and pack stock. Signing up with this type of outfit can turn out to be a dangerous ordeal! Earlier on these pages, I have listed where to write for information: game departments, U. S. Forest Service, and the ranchers and outfitters for trail rides.

In most states, a guide or packer is required to be registered. In all Forests and National Parks, he is also required to have a Special Use Permit to operate.

The Status of Your Guide Not all guides or outfitters have a Ph.D. after their names (but many do), and not all have college educations, but nevertheless, they are professionals in their line of endeavor; consequently, they should always be extended the respect due them.

What Is Expected of Both Outfitter and Guests

The Outfitter and His Service

Member-outfitters are experienced and reliable, with license and bond and a strict set of standards (outlined below). They are the top boss of the trip. Their services and camps vary with the individual. They usually provide a large cook tent with tables and seats where well balanced meals are served family-style. In cold seasons tents are heated and dry, and some have cots. The Outfitter's guides, wranglers, and cook are efficient and congenial, with proven ability. You are provided with a gentle mountain-trained horse and your gear and provisions for the entire journey are securely packed on pack animals. The first and last nights are usually spent at the Outfitter's ranch.

Outfitter's Standards

1. Members shall hold Class I Outfitters license, current for the year of operation, authorizing to outfit and/or pack for all types of hunting, fishing and sightseeing parties, using saddle and/or pack animals on a wilderness trip of two or more days.
2. Each member must have a permanent base of operation and own the majority of their pack and saddle stock and equipment for overnight camping.
3. Each base camp must meet these minimum requirements:
   a. A sanitary camp must be maintained at all times.
   b. Food—adequate, well prepared and cleanly served.
   c. Suitable latrine located properly from camp and trail.
   d. Adequate garbage disposal.
4. Each base camp shall have standard first aid kit. Spike camp—pocket kit.
5. Each member, his guide or packer must be able to maintain animals and gear and be able to pack.
6. Each member must use approved methods in care of trophies and meat.
7. Rates, services and accommodations shall be clearly defined to party *prior* to pack trip and available upon request.
8. Members shall stand inspection of their equipment by a three-member committee of the association.
9. Requirements of U. S. Forest Service and Montana

Fish and Game Commission shall be strictly adhered to.

10. Full cooperation between members of the Association prior use rights, camp site, grazing privileges and other existing practices of members shall be respected by fellow members.
11. Horses and equipment must be good, serviceable and adequate.
12. Members shall employ well trained, courteous and sufficient personnel to adequately care for guests.

Outfitters found in violation of Fish and Game Standards are subject to loss of license and expulsion as a member.

Code of Ethics for the Guest

If outfitters have a moral obligation, so does the guest. To make it easy on yourself and others, the following are the standards for the guest:

1. To travel well and get along with the rest of the party.
2. Guest must use care with outfitter's equipment and stock.
3. Guest should practice safety and must not sight in guns at the camp or hunting area.
4. Alcohol used in moderation is a social privilege.
5. Smokers should carefully discard cigarettes and matches. Do not litter trail with paper and trash.
6. Gun safety is a must. Identify your game to avoid accident or waste.
7. The guest should show the willingness and ability to make the stalk and kill.
8. Guests should respect outfitter's or guide's knowledge of country and game habits of the area.
9. Guests must respect outfitter's requirements for deposit and cancellation deadline.

Picking a good outfitter is an important part of planning a wilderness trip. Glidden McNeal (left) is taking this party on a hunting expedition.

The outfitter's services include wholesome meals three times a day. This family group has been hunting in the Ocala National Forest, Florida. (U.S. Forest Service photo.)

REMEMBER: You're in "God's Country," respect His laws of nature. The fish and game kill is only a part of the trip.

When to Plan Your Trip Contacts to outfitters should be made by February and firm bookings and deposits made by March or April. Most outfitters have return customers, and some are filled by early spring.

Where to Write for Information Select one or more outfitters from the area you wish to visit and write directly to the outfitter as each outfitter does his own booking. Ask the outfitter for his brochure or letter describing his services, equipment, provisions, area of trip, type of camp, specific type clothing and gear needed, dates available, prices, and application form. Cost of the trip will vary with outfitters and services. Prices range up and down from $35.00 per day. Hunting rates are usually higher than summer rates. This includes all but personal gear (horses, camp equipment, food, guide service, etc.).

Recommended Reading For detailed information on all types of hunting and weapons, read *The Hunter's Bible* (see bibliography).

Hunters, Keep This in Mind! Long since driven from city streets by motor vehicles, the horse ranks as the most practical mode of transportation for much Western big-game hunting. In return for serving the hunter, the horse demands more in cooperation and know-how than any motor vehicle.

Hunter Mort Proctor of Vermont and his Alaska-born guide, Larry Roberts, with a 65-inch spread of Alaska moose antlers in their hunting camp—an example of the good hunting in Alaska.

8

The Last Frontier— The Adventure of a Lifetime!

Alaska Ho! At last the Texans will have to tip their hats to the Alaskans, for Alaska outshines Texas in size, game, untapped resources—and in National Forests and Parks! Alaska is BIG! It's a riding, packing, big-game country!

Very few outdoorsmen realize the vastness of this last frontier. A map of Alaska superimposed on a map of the first 48 States shows Alaska's size in relation to the rest of the Union. Alaska is as large as Texas, California and Montana together (a total of 586,400 square miles) with a coastline longer than all of the first 48 states.

The state capital, Juneau, is further from Dutch Harbor than New York City is from San Francisco. It is almost as far from Juneau to the northernmost Point Barrow as it is from Seattle to the Mexican border.

The Big National Forests Alaska contains two of the largest national forests and two of the largest units of the national park system, from which wildlife overflows into these forests—a bonus for the big-game hunter! Alaska is a storehouse of recreational opportunities! In this relatively new state, with less than one percent of the total national population, there is 31 percent of the land in the National Park System, 65 percent of the wildlife refuge land, 64 percent of the public domain (Bureau of Land Management), and 11 percent of the National Forests acreage! It's big and it's wild!

Enchantment! Here is a part of the world apart held in the spell of its own majesty and mystery. Even the rollers of the Pacific are stilled to a respectful calm by the grandeur of the coastal and inland ranges.

A dream? Say, rather a dream for a packhorse safari, for this is the sensation that beguiles the traveler entering this vast wilderness land by air, land, or sea!

Big-Game Country This is big-game country inhabited by the giant Alaska brown bear, grizzly, black, and the rare "blue glacier" bear. The lordly moose, musk-ox, caribou, blacktail and Sitka deer, and the nimble-footed sheep and mountain goat (many trophy size) roam free. Ducks and geese are abundant—and don't forget that there are fighting salmon in the sea. Licensed guide service is excellent, too!

Alaxsxaq Alaxsxaq is the Aleut name for this vast recreational wonderland, one fifth as large as the other 49 states, easily reached by the Alaska Highway (formerly called "Alcan"), by private transportation, by aircraft or by boat. No matter how you travel, the scenery along the way is spectacular! The "Great Land" is so big, so completely full of surprises at every turn of a waterway, road, or trail, that you'll be spellbound by its sheer beauty and the scope and variety of its grandeur. Here are the tallest mountains on the North American Continent, glittering blue-green glaciers, and thousands of square miles of wilderness. It is a land of contrasts, a camera-bug's delight and a hunter's bonanza, teeming with ducks, geese, and big game!

The Largest National Forest Tongass National Forest comprises 16,016,140 acres (25,025+ square miles), and is the largest of the 154 national forests in the United States. The North Division has headquarters at Juneau 99801, and the South Division has headquarters at Ketchikan 99901.

Chugach National Forest This third national forest is located at Anchorage 99501. Like the Tongass, it also teems with wildlife. Once you leave town, you are in the wilderness. This forest consists of 4,726,145 acres (7,384+ square miles), and is the second largest national forest in the system.

Mount McKinley National Park 1,939,493 acres (3,030 square miles), is the largest of our National Parks. Headquarters: Mount McKinley Park, Alaska 99755. Hunting is done only with a camera in this park, but fishing is allowed. There are 93 miles of gravel surfaced roads in and accessible from the park and 20 miles of trails for hiking and trail riding—the rest is wilderness! The Denali Highway, a 156-mile road, connects the park road with the Richardson Highway, making the park accessible to private automobiles. Visitors can transport their automobiles to the park by train from Seward, Anchorage, or Fairbanks. Aircraft can be chartered from these towns. Naturalist and interpretive talks are presented at the Eielson Visitor Center during the day and at the hotel in the park in the evening.

The season is from June 1 to September 15. Daylight generally lasts more than 18 hours, and temperatures range from 30 to 40 degrees. Primitive, wild and breathtakingly beautiful, this gem of an area is 3,030 square miles of primeval wilderness in south central

Alaska. Besides Mount McKinley, 20,320 feet in elevation and the highest peak in North America, there is Mount Forsaker at 17,400 feet, Silvertone at 13,220 feet, and several other peaks at over 12,000 feet. This park is one of the largest game refuges in the United States. Among the 130 species of birds and 36 kinds of mammals, several species of fish make their homes here.

Katmai National Monument 2,697,590 acres (4,215 square miles) of wilderness. Headquarters: Mount McKinley Park, Alaska 99755. This is the largest area administered by the National Park Service. It is a dying volcanic region, and includes the famous "Valley of Ten Thousand Smokes," scene of a violent eruption in 1912. Although the monument is an outstanding exhibit of volcanism, it is also noted for its superlative scenery and wildlife. Waterfowl and fish are abundant here and the most prominent mammal is the Alaska brown bear. This animal, weighing from 1,000 to 1,800 pounds, is the largest carnivore in the world.

Camping is permitted upon receipt of a fire permit from a park ranger. Northern Consolidated Airlines, Inc., operatès two summer fishing camps within the monument at Naknek Lake and Lake Grosvenor. Information and reservations are available from Northern Consolidated Airlines, Inc., Anchorage, Alaska 99501. Bush-piloted planes may also be chartered to this and other wilderness areas.

Glacier Bay National Monument 2,274,595 acres (3,554+ square miles) of wilderness. Headquarters: Box 1781, Juneau, Alaska 99801. Glacier Bay is the second largest monument in the National Park System. Great tidewater glaciers, an exhibit of early stages of post-glacial forests, and rare species of wildlife are the main attractions. (Blue glacier bear are found here.)

An Alaska Brown Bear, shot first with a camera and then with a rifle, joins the other wild game which has provided superb hunting for sportsmen from the U.S. and abroad.

The main features are the 20 tremendous glaciers and many lesser ones; Mt. Fairweather, rising 15,320 feet; and Glacier Bay. The Bay, about 50 miles long and 2½ to 10 miles wide, was filled with ice some 3,000 feet thick as recently as 250 years ago. Glacier Bay lies between two parallel mountain ranges loftier than any in the United States outside of Alaska. The eastern peaks belong to the ice-draped St. Elias Range, largely unmapped and unexplored, which reaches its climax 140 miles northwest of the monument in 18,000 foot Mount St. Elias. The southeast end of the monument, toward the mouth of Glacier Bay, is clothed in moss-draped spruce and hemlock. Glacier Bay and Sitka National Monuments are under the immediate supervision of the Superintendent, National Park Service, U. S. Department of the Interior, Box 1781, Juneau, Alaska 99801.

Sitka National Monument 54.33 acres. Headquarters: Sitka, Alaska 99835. While this monument is one of the smaller ones in the Park System, it is big in Alaskan history. Sitka is one of the marine gateways to wilderness backcountry. Here you can see replicas of old Russian fortifications, Russian Orthodox church icons, and old pioneer homes. At the Monument visitor center there are exhibits, films, scenic trails, and totem poles. Sitka is the site of the Indian stockades where the Kik-Siti tribe made their last stand against Russian settlers.

How to Get to The Land of the Midnight Sun The Alaska Highway runs about 1,200 miles, through Canada to the Alaskan border, less than 300 miles south of the Arctic Circle. Or you can turn south at Haines Junction to reach southeast Alaska.

The Marine Highway From Kelsey Bay, British Columbia, you can board the British Columbian ocean-going ferry *Prince Rupert* and travel over 330 miles of ocean freeway to Prince Rupert, British Columbia, where connections are made with the Alaska Marine Highway State Ferries that connect with ports along the Alaska coast. The ferries transport 100 automobiles and from 400 to 500 passengers.

The Inside Passage This passage is a thousand mile long waterway protected on both sides by land, including beautiful islands, endless forests, fantastic mountains dropping to the water's edge, and occasionally icebergs and glaciers—an ideal locale for the small-craft boat enthusiast. The scenic grandeur of the Inside Passage offers the vacationer and sportsman some of the world's most dramatic scenery and hunting.

The Alaska Highway (Formally called the Alcan, a shortening for Alaska-Canada during World War II.) The Long Road! Access by road to Alaska—the last frontier—is by 1,523-miles of gravel and blacktop highway from Dawson Creek, British Columbia, to Fairbanks, Alaska.

What Will It Cost? Hotel and motel rates are comparable to those elsewhere in the United States and Canada. Meals and food prices vary, and are usually somewhat higher since it is a long haul to this northernmost state. Air transport is inexpensive, considering the distance involved. Charter flights average $35 per hour and up, but an hour's flight covers a lot of territory! Gasoline costs 40 to 60 cents per gallon. State ferries run $30 per passenger over the entire route from Prince Rupert to Skagway and $99 per car. Guides for big-game hunting run about $50 to $150 per day, the latter including lodging or boat charter, meals, and many extras.

A typical hunting safari to Alaska from central California costs approximately $500 per person, plus a few extra dollars for film, curios, etc. Five of my Sonora, California, neighbors decided not to hunt the nearby Sierra Nevada range, and took a hunting jaunt to the far north. The party left the Sonora foothills in two camper-pickups and drove north to Prince Rupert, deep in British Columbia, then ferried north for 40 hours via the marine highway through the Inside Passage to Haines, just below Skagway. From there they drove 500 miles to their chosen hunting grounds in Units 11, 12, and 13 near Nabena in the Wrangell mountains of the Alaska Range, 200 miles northwest of Anchorage. Hunting was excellent and the hunters collected moose, deer, bear, and caribou.

Two days after their arrival, due to urgent business in Sonora, three of the party flew from Anchorage to San Francisco and home. This left "Papa Joe" Sciaroni, the leader of the party, alone at Grizzly Lake with his camper. Joe, known in Sonora as the "Great White Hunter," wanted to spend several weeks in Arctic research. Later Joe flew back to Sonora to spend Thanksgiving with his friends and family, then he returned to Alaska (this was an extra cost) and drove his camper home with his trophies. The hunting party left most of the meat at an orphanage in Alaska.

Where to Write for Full Details About Alaska

Division of Tourism and Economic Development, P.O. Box 2391, Juneau, Alaska 99801

Chamber of Commerce, Fairbanks, Alaska

U.S. Bureau of Land Management, Department of the Interior, Juneau, Alaska 99801

Forest Supervisor (North Unit), Tongass National Forest, U.S. Department of Agriculture, P.O. Box 1049, Juneau, Alaska 99801

Forest Supervisor (South Unit), Tongass National Forest, U.S. Department of Agriculture, P.O. Box 2278, Ketchikan, Alaska 99901

Superintendent, Mt. McKinley National Park, McKinley Park, Alaska 99755

Superintendent, Katmai Nat'l Mon., National Park Service, Department of the Interior, McKinley Park, Alaska 99755

Glacier Bay & Sitka Nat'l Monuments, National Park Service, U.S. Department of the Interior, Juneau, Alaska 99801

Alaska Department of Fish & Game, Subport Building, Juneau, Alaska 99801

Roads & Ferries, Department of Public Works, Juneau, Alaska 99801

Supervisory Park Historian, Sitka National Monument, National Park Service, Department of the Interior, Sitka, Alaska 99835

Canadian Information

British Columbia Government Travel Bureau, Victoria, British Columbia, Canada

Yukon Travel Bureau, Whitehorse, Yukon Territory, Canada

Canadian Government Travel Bureau, Ottawa, Ontario, Canada

Canadian Government Travel Bureau, Canada House, 608 Fifth Avenue, New York, N. Y. 10020

Canadian Government Travel Bureau, 102 West Monroe Street (Corner of Clark Street), Chicago, Illinois 60606

Canadian Government Travel Bureau, 1 Second Street (Corner of Market St.), San Francisco, California

On horseback or on foot, the Chilkoot Pass trail of gold rush fame offers the outdoorsman one of Alaska's most pleasurable wilderness experiences. The trail, cleared and maintained by the State Parks and Recreation Branch, begins near the ghost town of Dyea near Skagway.

Northwest Territories Tourist Office, Kent-Albert Building, Ottawa, Ontario, Canada

National Parks of Canada, Canadian Government Travel Bureau, Ottawa, Ontario, Canada

These agencies do an excellent job of public relations and send many brochures, maps, and information on where to go and what to see! So, if you want to enjoy a really big wilderness adventure, try Alaska next time!

Sturdy, waterproof boots such as these are a must for the outdoorsman. (Browning Boots.)

9

Boots, Saddles, Packs and Hitches

Boots Riding or cowboy type boots are fine to wear on park bridle paths or for cattle ranch work, and even if you just trail ride and don't do much walking in remote backcountry. Searching for grazing stock in the morning can be rough on your feet if you use the pointed-toed high-heeled cowboy boot! Nevertheless, I have seen many packers wear a sturdy six or eight-inch hiking boot with a non-skid sole with a semi-high woodsman's heel. Since high rocky mountains are rough, and one has to do some walking, these are ideal for both hiking and horse hunting.

To Prevent Becoming Saddle Sore To keep from getting too weary and saddle sore on a long day's ride, you should get off once in a while and walk a few hundred yards to keep limbered up. Also it is much safer to get off and walk and lead your mount up and down very steep terrain, and even on level slippery granite stretches.

The Riding Saddle Every camper or sportsman who has ridden the high trails or hunted game on horseback knows that outfitters furnish saddles. But any sportsman or trail rider who has used one of these provided rigs will agree that they leave something to be desired in the way of riding comfort.

For the person who goes on a once-in-a-lifetime packhorse jaunt, a personal saddle is a needless luxury. For the trail rider or hunter who rides with any degree of regularity, owning a well-fitted saddle can supply an extra margin of comfort.

How to Sit Tall in the Saddle A good heavy-duty stock saddle will, with reasonable care, give a lifetime of satisfaction and can be purchased for $150 to $200. You should buy with the same caution that you would use in the purchase of any fine piece of equipment. (Note stock saddle illustration.)

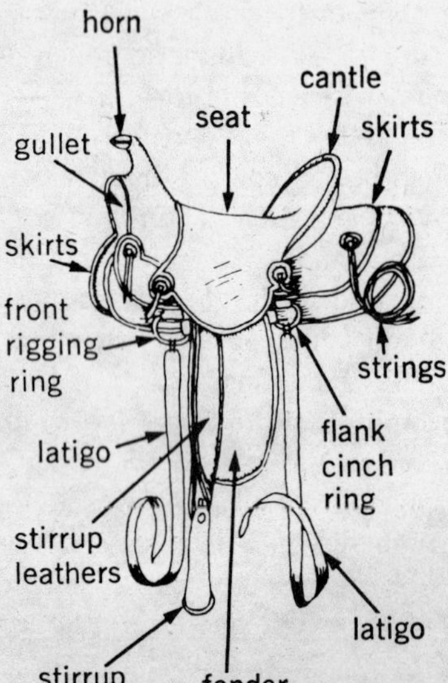

Stock saddle.

The Sawbuck Pack Saddle In this discussion, the general principles apply to any pack saddle when packing horses, mules, or donkeys. The sawbuck saddle is usually made of birch, and consists of two side boards, shaped to fit the animal's back on each side of the withers and backbone, and is firmly held together by rigid crosstrees at both ends. The sawbuck saddle comes in both single and double rig—the latter is equipped with two cinches. Both have a breast strap and breeching harness for rough terrain. This prevents the saddle

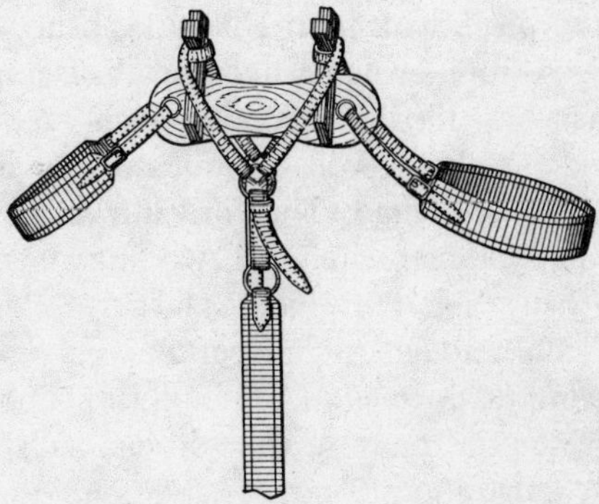

Full-rigged pack saddle (single rig).

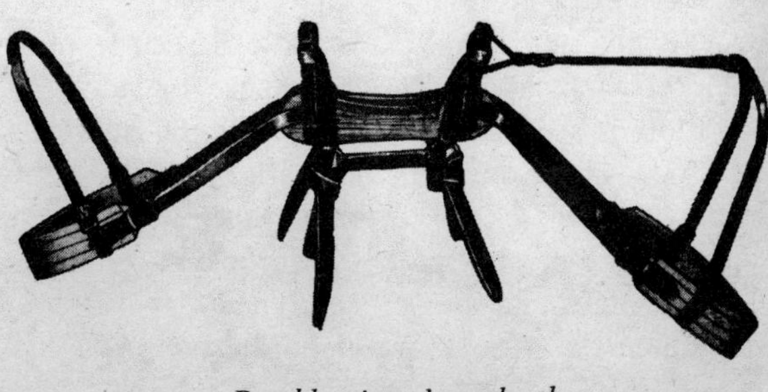

Double rigged sawbuck.

and load from slipping when negotiating steep trails. It should fit the particular animal on which it is used, although with thick blankets or pads an accurate fit is not always necessary. The sweat blanket or corona next to the skin should be of wool or hair and should be kept clean, free from wrinkles, and as dry as possible. Breast straps and breeching should be snug, but not tight, and once adjusted, need not be changed unless used on another pack animal. The saddle is removed by unfastening only the nigh (left) end of the breast strap and the nigh side latigos which adjust the tightness of the cinches. When saddling, the saddle can be swung into place with the right hand, using the left to keep latigos from swinging underneath. Before tightening the cinches, tilt the saddle an inch or two toward the off side so that it will be brought into line by the final pull on the latigo. The forward cinch should be tight so that you can barely get two fingers between the animal's belly and the cinch. The rear cinch should only be snug enough to prevent the saddle from tipping forward on down grades, and must be loose enough so that it doesn't interfere with the animal's breathing. (Note the illustrations of single- and double-rigged sawbuck saddles.)

The Decker Pack Saddle In the Northwest, the U.S. Forest Service and some pack stations seem to favor the Decker pack saddle. The "sawbuck" or "crosstree" pack saddle is seen more in California, the Southwest, and Mexico. However, both the Park and Forest Services use the sawbuck in several of their regions, and the crosstree is most popular with packers throughout the nation. It might be added that it is also much cheaper than the other more elaborate types.

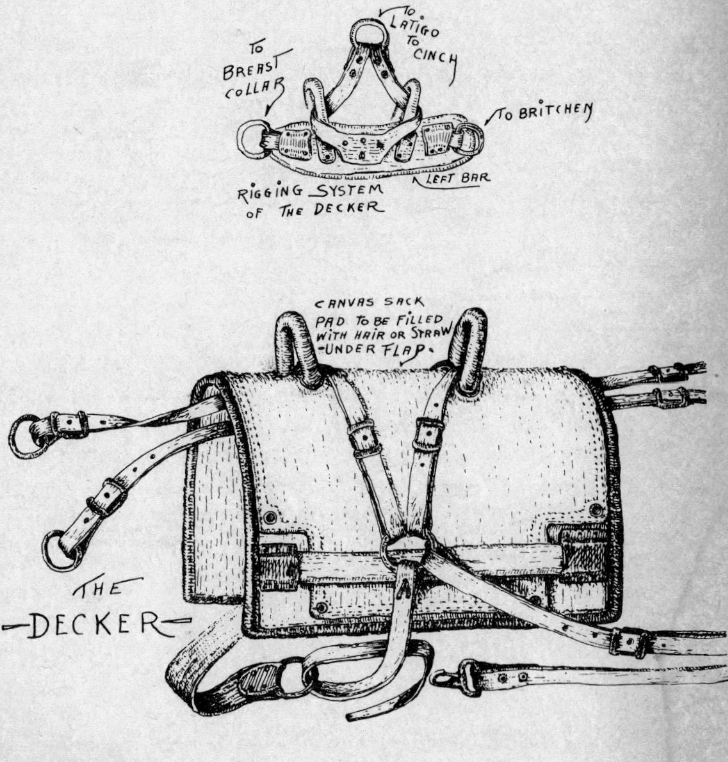

Decker saddle.

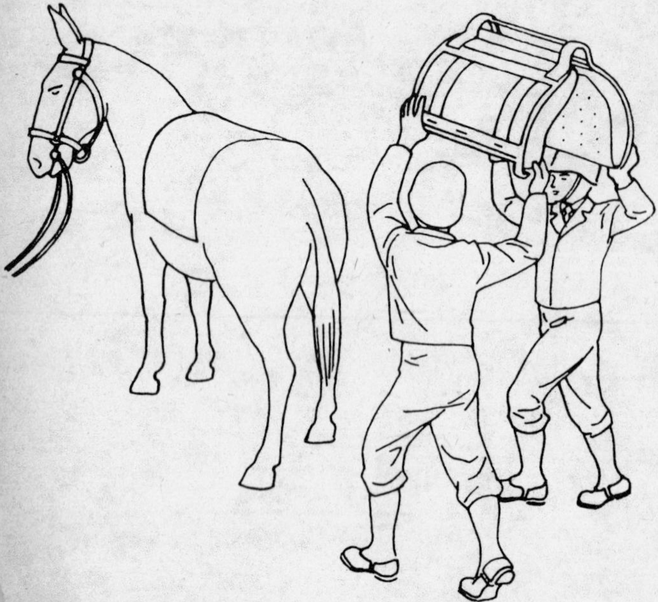

Packers lifting a Phillips Army pack saddle prior to setting it on the animal's back.

Off packer taking up slack while near packer pulls down on the load, using a single diamond hitch.

The Phillips Pack Saddle The United States Army prefers the Phillips pack saddle. This cargo pack saddle weighs 95 pounds—quite a load for a pack animal when it is loaded down with a 150 pound pack load, plus the saddle! The Phillips is an elaborate metal and leather outfit. It takes two packers to place it on a pack animal. I have seen several for sale in surplus stores along with the Army McClellan riding saddle.

The Army McClellan Saddle After the National Park Service took over jurisdiction from the Army in 1916, the U. S. Park Rangers were issued McClellan saddles until about 1935, when stock saddles were furnished.

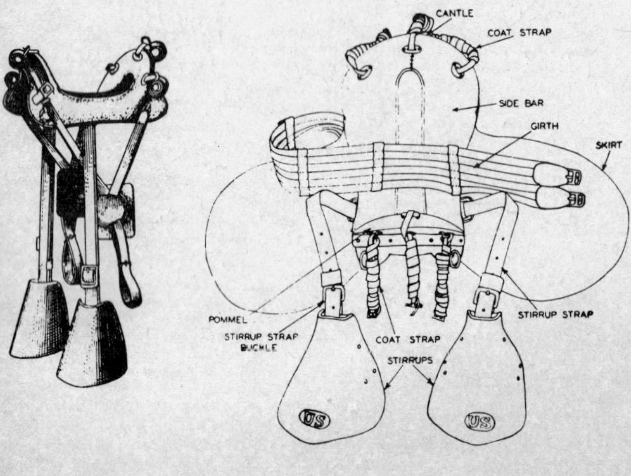

McClellan military saddle.

For many years I have enjoyed using this lightweight saddle, with its many straps that you can use to fasten on your rain slicker, extra blankets, and other equipment. I have even used it for a pack saddle when my sawbuck was in for repairs. For high elevation patrol or trail riding, it can't be beat for ease for both man and beast. A heavy stock saddle of 45 pounds or more plus a 175 pound man can be tough on a horse traveling the rough rocky trails in high mountain terrain.

I use my McClellan saddle when traveling along the John Muir Trail in California, where some trails and passes reach a sky-level elevation of over 13,000 feet, and I use my stock saddle for lower elevation hunting trips.

The author using an Army McClellan riding saddle for a pack saddle.

The Tenderfoot Packer A tenderfoot packer and an inexperienced or poorly broken pack animal make an unsafe combination. If you are not an old hand at handling stock and packing, insist that the pack station gives you a gentle animal.

Ask Your Packer Questions Have the packer give you information on any unusual traits the animal he rents you might have. Have him show you how to properly adjust the pack saddle and blankets.

Make certain that the pack saddle fits properly. A long, narrow-treed saddle will injure the back of a fat, short-coupled horse or mule, and a wide, flat saddle should not be put on a narrow-backed animal. Use plenty of hair and wool pads and blankets under a pack saddle to properly protect the animal's back. Be sure that the padding is wrinkle-free and that no abrasive debris is under it.

Packing Cargo on a Riding Saddle Riding saddles are often used as emergency pack saddles. With the exception of the flat English riding saddle, which makes a poor substitute, any riding saddle can be readily packed by using a 30 foot pack rope to form a basket sling. The center of the rope is secured to the front arch or horn of the saddle and arranged as shown in the illustration. The loads are placed on the saddle in either a vertical or horizontal position. They are secured as in the basket hitch, except that no quarter ropes are drawn from under the standing ropes. The running end is tied to the standing rope with a sliding clove-hitch.

When the pack is loaded in such fashion a manty covers it, and then one of the Diamond type hitches is used to lash down the whole load securely.

Saddling Up—the Right Way How to prevent sore backs: first of all, a saddle or pack animal's back must be kept clean. A curry comb and brush are a "must"

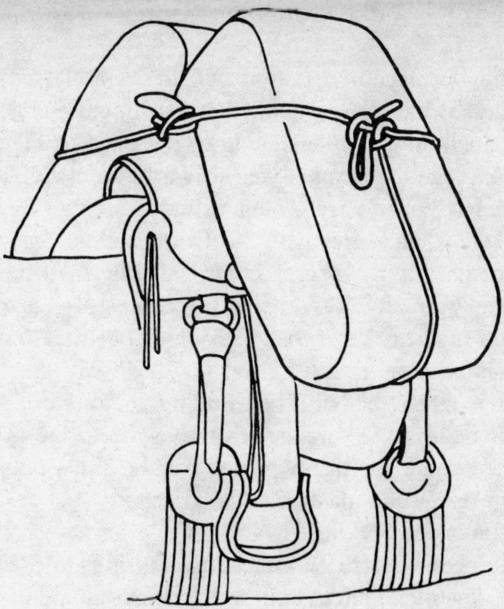

Packing a riding saddle.

to keep an animal clean and well-groomed. When using these grooming tools, be gentle, especially at tender points. However, to save time when in the field on a pack trip many horsemen just use a piece of burlap sacking to wipe their animal's back clean before saddling, and only curry when conditions call for a more thorough job.

Many sore backs are caused by improperly adjusted, wrinkled or dirty saddle pads and blankets. Some blankets are sold in what is called "single-fold or "two-fold." You can also use a regular sized wool blanket by using the Army fold. Take a full-sized blanket and fold it lengthwise once, then crosswise in even thirds, making six thicknesses of blanket. The pad or blanket should be placed so that it will fit squarely under the saddle so that pressure will be distributed evenly from the backbone down each side of the edge of the saddle skirts. Place the blanket well forward, then slide it back so that it is properly seated, with about two inches of blanket or pad ahead of the front saddle skirts. This will comb the hair back so that it will lie smoothly. The front margin should come to the center of the withers.

Too many riders, when they find that they have put the saddle blanket a little too far back, will pull it forward where it should be. Pulling it forward in this manner turns the hair the wrong way, and the pressure of the saddle on those places causes "hot-spots" and the start of some nasty saddle sores.

Positioning a Saddle Many times I have seen a rider walk up to a horse or mule dragging a saddle, only to have a gentle, quiet, and well-mannered animal start backing and sidling nervously, rolling his eyes, snorting, and laying his ears back. I have seen this same swashbuckling TV cowboy type slap on a saddle blanket, then grab his saddle with a mighty roundhouse swing, heave it in the general direction of the animal, stirrups and cinches flying. The cinch ring comes down on the off side of the animal with a vicious whack on the shins, and the stirrups clout the animal's ribs—and when they hit, they hurt. No wonder the poor beast gets spooky!

To prevent this punishment, lift the cinch gently back over the saddle on the animal's back. When mounted, push the cinch and stirrup down on the off side.

Use Care—Animals Have Feelings Too! Too much stress cannot be put on the proper positioning of any riding or pack saddle and the correct adjustment! The forward edge of the saddle should be sufficiently in back of the shoulder blades so that it doesn't dig into them and will allow them to operate freely. A clearance of two or three inches is usually about right. The saddle should not be canted to either side.

I find that it is much quicker and easier to put both blanket and saddle slightly high on the withers, then get hold of the rear of the blanket at the center, and slide both blanket and saddle back until the saddle sits where it naturally should be—in the hollow just behind the withers. Next, I grasp the saddle blanket front and rear along the animal's backbone and lift it about an inch. This makes a small tunnel of air under the blanket in the midline which provides ventilation and prevents the saddle load from rubbing along the backbone.

Cinch Adjustment A saddle covers so great an area of moving surface that proper cinching is vital. Excessive binding of the front cinch may injure the animal's back and sides, interfere with breathing, or cause galls and swellings. The long strap used to secure the cinch is called the latigo. One either reaches under the belly of the animal or, when packing, the off-side packer pushes the cinch under the belly to the near-side packer, who passes the latigo through the cinch ring from inside out and then continues through the ring on the saddle rigging from outside in. This is repeated to give two complete loops with the latigo, the second loop being over the first in the rings rather than beside it. The forward edge of the cinch MUST not be less than three inches from the front leg when the animal stands straight so that it will not pinch the skin when he walks, as otherwise cinch sores will occur and they are very difficult to heal. The loops made with the latigo provide enough friction to hold as the cinch tightens. The rear cinch must not be as tight as the front cinch, because the rear of the saddle covers the area of greatest motion, the flexible short-ribbed region, and the tender area over the kidneys. Since the hind legs are the propelling members, the hind quarters move side to side and up and down. These movements must not be restricted by cinch pressure. There must be no interference with locomotion or with the animal's breathing with a too tight rear cinch.

The exact amount of cinch pressure required can be determined only by experience. A safe rule of thumb to follow is to give the front cinch pressure sufficient to hold the saddle solidly in place, but not so tight that you can't get two fingers between the animal's chest and the cinch. The rear cinch should only be cinched tightly enough to limit the rock motions of the saddle and to help prevent the rear of the saddle from tipping up or slipping forward. Never have the rear cinch so tight that your whole hand cannot be slipped under it. In testing cinch pressure, the fingers or hand should be inserted from rear to front so that when withdrawn the hair will not be ruffled. Ruffled hair can cause galls! (Note the illustrations of latigo ties.) I personally prefer the double half hitch with a loop, sometimes called the Arizona hitch. It can be unhitched more quickly.

The Cargo Pack Some "dude" campers and fishermen want all the modern conveniences of home when they hit the trail, and a packer will load anything a horse or mule can carry to make his client happy—gas refrigerators, cook stoves, small boats—you name it and the outfitter will try and get it into the woods for you. Of course, more packaged cargo means more pack animals will be involved, and that puts more money in the jeans of the outfitter. To me, that just doesn't seem like camping!

Some years ago, I was assigned as a staff Ranger to assist Mrs. Eleanor Roosevelt on a week's pack trip in

Preparing supplies for loading.

Yosemite National Park. I thought I had seen everything when I saw the government packer loading a collapsible latrine that folded "U" shape on a mule. I bet there were 15 hinges on the contraption. It even had a plywood door! However, she never made use of it, and the packer finally ditched it over a bluff.

Maurice Fickes and Joel Frykman showing the correct way to pack for a wilderness trip. (U.S. Forest Service photo.)

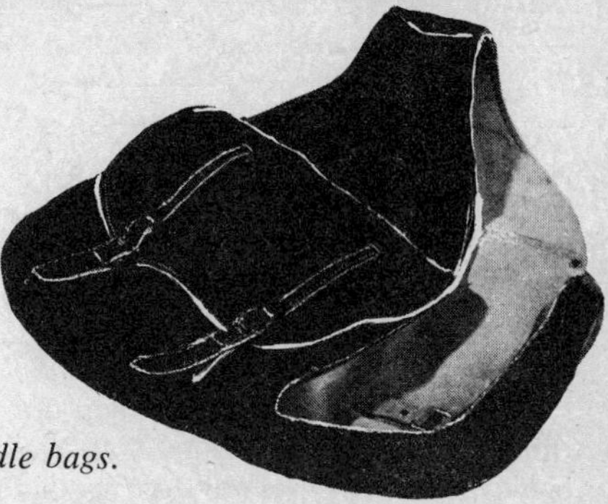

Saddle bags.

Canvas kyacks.

Packing the Sawbuck Normally, the sawbuck saddle requires the use of matched box kyacks or leather or canvas panniers, which when packed must have a difference of not over one or two pounds in weight. I usually use a small spring scale to weigh the cargo so that I can keep loads down around 150 to 185 pounds. Some packers simply will not allow a pack load heavier than 140 pounds per animal in rough country. Sometimes cargo is carried in slings with the sawbuck saddle.

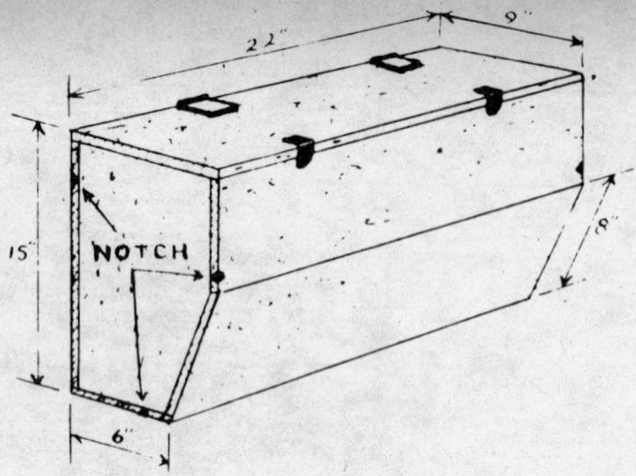

Pannier. The dimensions shown are those of the best panniers. The lash ropes that secure the pannier on the sawbuck saddle fit into the notches on the front edges.

Packaging Cargo for the Decker Saddle Generally, panniers are not used with Decker saddles. All loads are packaged-up in cargo loads instead, matched as evenly as possible, and lashed to the saddle with sling ropes looped through the iron rings and fastened with the "Decker Hitch." The whole cargo is then covered with a manty and lashed down with one of the varied diamond hitches. One of the virtues of the Decker is that loads of uneven shapes may be packed, since they do not have to fit inside panniers or box type kyacks. Home-made kyacks can be lashed onto a Decker saddle if hardwood cleats are provided at each end of the kyack box. If cleats are not provided the box must be wrapped in a canvas manty and hung on the saddle with a box or basket hitch.

The Pack Hitches The one-man diamond hitch is generally preferred because it can be used when packing alone and is just as quick and secure as any other hitch. Nevertheless, there are several types of diamond hitches such as the so-called Government diamond, Wyoming diamond, double diamond, etc. The novice

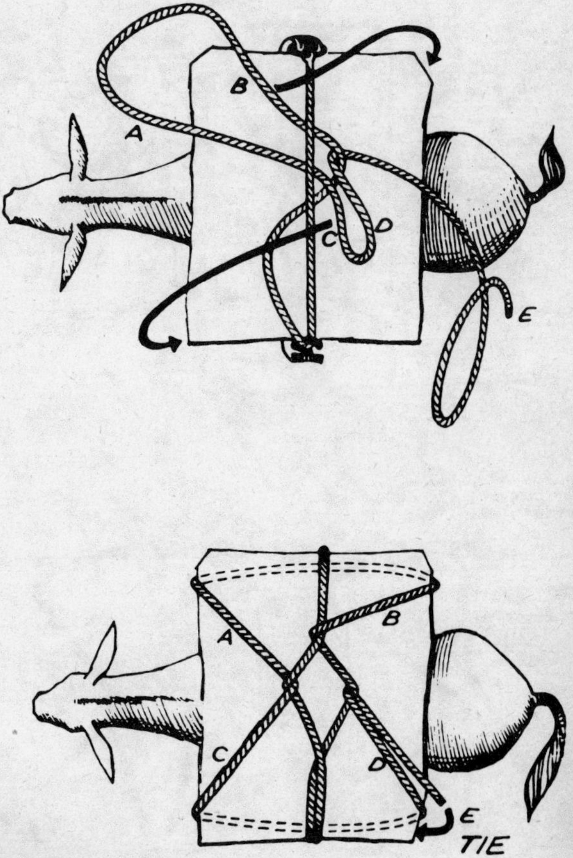

One man or Government Diamond hitch.
From All About Camping *by W. K. Merrill, The Stackpole Company, Harrisburg, Pennsylvania.*

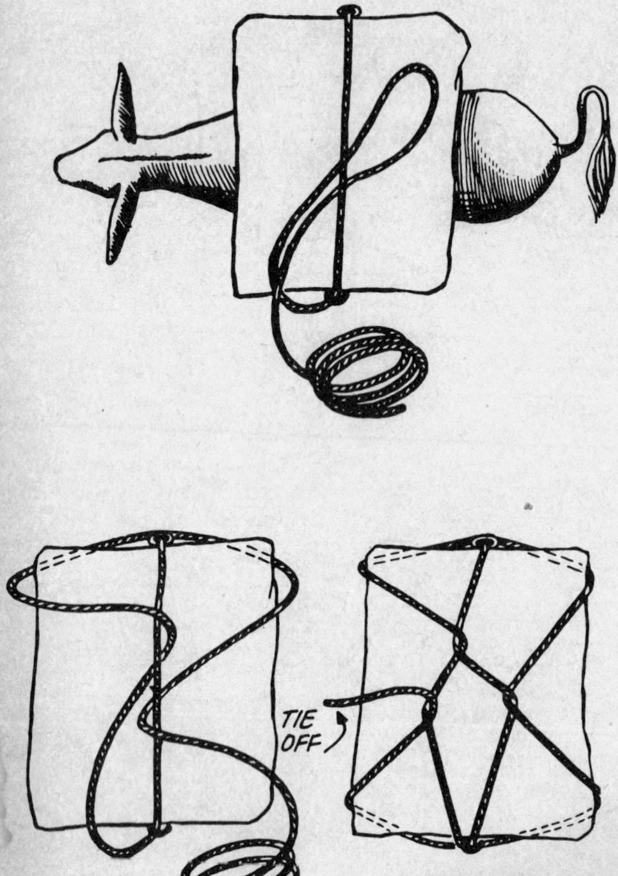

Lone Ranger hitch.
From All About Camping *by W. K. Merrill, The Stackpole Company, Harrisburg, Pennsylvania.*

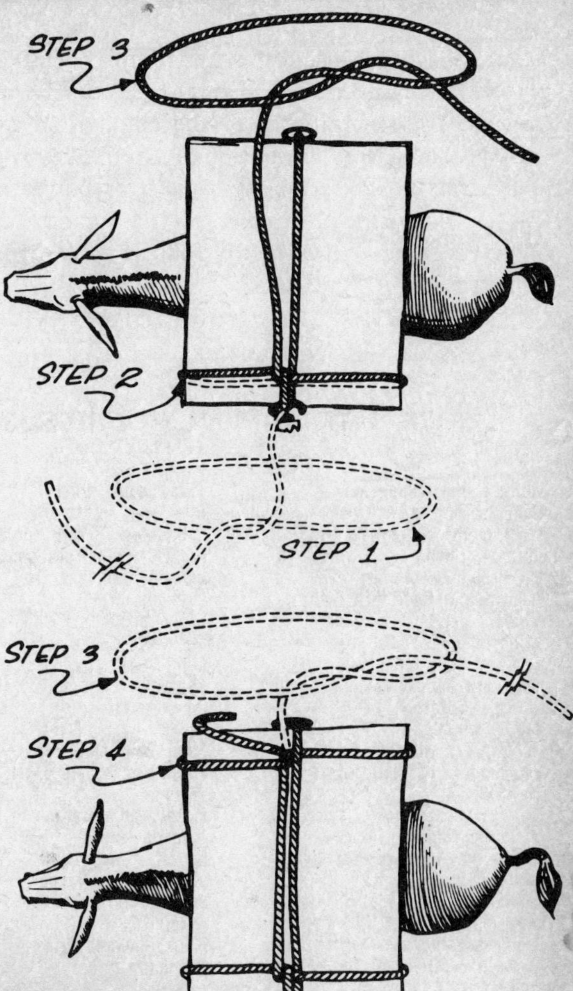

Box hitch.
From All About Camping *by W. K. Merrill, The Stackpole Company, Harrisburg, Pennsylvania.*

packer will probably find it easier to use a squaw hitch or the Lone Ranger hitch. However, it can be fun to learn and use several hitches—the mark of an experienced packer! (Note illustrations.)

Hitches for Burros The pack outfit for burros is the same as for horses or mules—only in smaller size. If you can pack a burro correctly, you can pack the larger animals, too!

PACK OUTFIT EQUIPMENT CHECKLIST

Personal Gear
- Toilet kit
- Hunting and fishing license
- Compass and maps
- Wash cloths and towels

Clothing — Inner
- Lightweight wool shirt
- Heavyweight wool shirt
- Medium weight wool pants
- Wool underwear (2)
- Socks, 6 pr., wool
- Bandanna handkerchiefs

Clothing — Outer
- Saddle slicker
- Hunting cap with ear flaps
- Red hunting hat with brim
- Down jacket
- Wool cruiser coat
- Mountain climbing boots
- Barker (or Sno-Paks) boots
- Rain parka and pants
- Leather work gloves
- Wool mittens
- Suspenders
- Camp moccasins

Miscellaneous
- Sun glasses (yellow lens)
- Binoculars
- Spotting scope, small tripod
- Extra inner-soles
- Extra bulbs and batteries
- Flashlight
- Pocket knife (BSA model)
- Sheath knife ($3\frac{1}{2}$-inch blade)
- Waterproofed matches

Firearms Gear
- Rifle, scope-sighted
- Rifle, iron sights or Shotgun (if bird hunting)
- Hooded leather scabbard
- Cleaning kit, firearms
- Ammunition
- Scope hoods

Camp Gear
- Light canvas fly, 12 x 12 ft.
- Tarpaulin, canvas, 10 x 10 ft.
- Coleman lantern
- Axe, single-bit 3 lbs. head
- Camp saw, folding
- White gas, square 5 gal. can
- Strainer
- Extra generators and mantles for lantern
- Shovel, forester type 3 lbs.
- 50 ft. $\frac{1}{2}$-inch rope
- Ball twine
- Toilet tissue
- Pliers, lineman type
- Aluminum grill
- Wire grill
- Reflector oven
- Pressure cooker (optional) Cooking pans
- Kettles
- Kitchen gear, knives, forks, spoons, pancake turner, etc.
- Tableware
- Bottle and can-opener

Battery-powered shaver
Hot-water bag or bottle
Thermos bottle (qt. size)
Sharpening stone
Boot waterproofing
First-aid kit
Personal medicines
Smoking gear and tobacco
Pocket warmer
Flannel pajamas
Hooded sweatshirt and pants
Air mattress
Down sleeping bag
Bed roll
Air pump
Camera, extra film, and gear
Duffel bags
Saddle bags
Snake bite kit
Waterproof match safe

Aluminum foil
Lunch gear, wax paper, sacks
Salt and pepper shakers
Soap and dish towels, detergents
Kitchen Maid, S.O.S. pads
Pot holders
Paper towels
Large cooking fork
Dutch oven
Large iron fry pan
Nesting cook kit
Coffee pot
Dish pan
Wash pan
Oil cloth
Plates
Cups
Butcher knife
Paring knife
Insect repellent

EQUIPMENT CHECK-LIST FOR FAMILY CAMPING

- ______ TENT
- ______ POLES
- ______ STAKE BAG AND STAKES
- ______ ROPE AND AXE
- ______ FOLDING CHAIRS
- ______ SMALL BROOM
- ______ DUSTPAN
- ______ SHOVEL
- ______ CARD TABLE
- ______ LANTERN (EXTRA MANTLE)
- ______ TENT WARMER
- ______ FUEL FOR LIGHT AND HEAT
- ______ TARP
- ______ DETACHABLE CAR SPOTLIGHT
- ______ FLASHLIGHTS, BATTERIES
- ______ SMALL TENT RUG

SLEEPING EQUIPMENT

- ______ AIR MATTRESS
- ______ PUMP
- ______ CARRYING BAG FOR ABOVE
- ______ PILLOWS
- ______ SLEEPING BAG AND COVERS
- ______ GROUND CLOTH
- ______
- ______

HIKING EQUIPMENT

- ______ KNAPSACK
- ______ CANTEEN
- ______ TRAIL TENT
- ______ COMPASS
- ______ TRAIL STOVE
- ______ MESS KIT
- ______
- ______

FISHING TACKLE

- ______ RODS
- ______ REELS
- ______ TACKLE BOX (CHECK CONTENTS)
- ______ LANDING NET
- ______ BAIT BOX
- ______ HUNTING KNIFE
- ______ LIFE JACKETS
- ______ WADERS
- ______
- ______

TOOL KIT

- ______ HAMMER
- ______ PLIERS
- ______ SCREWDRIVER
- ______ NAILS
- ______ WIRE
- ______
- ______

PHOTOGRAPHIC EQUIPMENT

- ______ CAMERAS
- ______ FILM
- ______ LIGHT METER
- ______ AUXILIARY LENS
- ______ FILTERS AND ADAPTERS
- ______ CARRYING CASE
- ______ SUPPLY STORAGE BOX
- ______ TRIPOD

MISCELLANEOUS SUPPLIES

- ______ MAP AND MAP CASE
- ______ FIRST AID KIT
- ______ SNAKE BITE KIT
- ______ INSECT REPELLENT
- ______ BINOCULARS
- ______ BOOKS AND MAGAZINES
- ______ PAPER AND PENCILS
- ______ NOTEBOOK
- ______ STATIONERY AND STAMPS
- ______ SUNTAN LOTION
- ______ SEWING KIT
- ______ CARDS
- ______
- ______

CLOTHES AND PERSONAL ITEMS

- ______ ZIPPERED CARRYING BAG
- ______ UNDERWEAR
- ______ SOCKS
- ______ PAJAMAS
- ______ TROUSERS, JEANS, SHORTS
- ______ SHIRTS, BLOUSES, DRESSES
- ______ SHOES
- ______ SWEATERS, COATS
- ______ JACKETS
- ______ HATS OR CAPS
- ______ RAINCOAT AND BOOTS
- ______ SWIMMING SUITS

- ______ TOILET KIT
- ______ SHAVING KIT
- ______ TOOTH BRUSHES AND PASTE
- ______ LOTIONS AND CREAMS
- ______ BRUSH AND COMB
- ______ MIRROR
- ______ TOWEL AND WASH CLOTH
- ______ SOAP AND SOAP BOX
- ______ READING MATERIAL
- ______ LAUNDRY BAG
- ______ EYEGLASSES AND SUNGLASSES
- ______ HANDKERCHIEFS
- ______
- ______
- ______
- ______
- ______

COOKING EQUIPMENT

- ______ CAMP STOVE
- ______ ICE BOX
- ______ PLASTIC DISHPAN
- ______ SMALL AND LARGE FRYING PAN
- ______ 2 MEDIUM COOKING PANS
- ______ DISH TOWEL AND RAGS
- ______ LIQUID SOAP
- ______ CHORE BOY
- ______ THERMOS AND CLEANING BRUSH
- ______ NAPKINS AND PAPER TOWELS
- ______ PANCAKE TURNER
- ______ BUTCHER KNIFE AND PARING KNIFE
- ______ LONG FORK
- ______ HOT PADS
- ______ SERVING SPOONS
- ______ CAN AND BOTTLE OPENERS
- ______ LIDS
- ______ STORAGE JARS
- ______ MATCHES IN WATERPROOF BOX
- ______ SILVERWARE
- ______ PAPER PLATES
- ______ CUPS AND SAUCERS
- ______ SMALL BOWLS
- ______ SALT AND PEPPER SHAKERS
- ______ SUGAR SHAKER

Big appetites are the rule, not the exception, after a day's packing. (U.S. Forest Service photo.)

10

Trailside Camp Cookery–How to Eat Happily in the Woods!

The Planning Stage Those of you who have camped out before will recall that mealtime can include some of the best moments of a summer mountain vacation. A healthy appetite plus good nourishing food properly cooked can make for a happy hunting or fishing camp.

At home, you don't have to worry or think too much about what's cooking, since your wife or mother usually has the food ready at mealtime, unless you eat all your meals out.

If you hire a pack outfit, your packer will relieve you of the cooking and kitchen chores. With a small party you might even jump in and help out. Your packer or horse wrangler will appreciate extra help if you haven't a camp cook along. If you are using your own stock it will be a do-it-yourself deal. If you haven't had any camp cooking experience, your cooking may be rough on your stomach!

Going On Your Own If you outfit yourself with simple kitchen gear, with foods that will not spoil readily, if it will cook quickly, and can be handled easily on a camp griller on a sheepherder type stove or grilled over coals of a small cooking fire, you are in business.

First Things First! Well in advance of your proposed safari, you will have to make up a menu list that is satisfactory to all members of the party. This will mean a conference at someone's home so that food ideas may be exchanged and decided on, as well as who will do most of the cooking and is best qualified for the job. Then it is a matter of having the right amount and the right kind of food and necessary cooking gear on hand, knowing how to build a simple fireplace and make the right type of cooking fire for the meal you have planned, and to be able to cook and make the food tasty, not only for yourself, but for any companions who make the trek with you.

Making Up the Grub List This part can be fun for all those going on the pack safari. In making up a menu, figure out how many days you will be away, how many breakfasts, lunches, and suppers will be needed, and multiply this by the number of persons going on the trek. Add to this two or three basic staples for use in an emergency, and add 25 percent more of everything to be on the safe side. Remember that appetites in the high country increase tremendously when one is riding, fishing, or stalking game most of the day and a considerable amount of energy is expended. DON'T forget that you may have to lay over several days in case of storm. And DON'T forget that you feed the packer and any of his helpers that may be along! Since you burn up a lot of energy in this type of camping, don't forget to bring plenty of energy sweets such as hard candies, jams, jellies, and honey! The invigorating cold clear

Dinner is served in an individual mess kit.

air sparks one's sweet tooth! Someone in your party may be on a non-cholesterol or slimming diet, so you must provide for them and even let them cook their own meals if necessary. It will be much easier on everyone's stomach if you stay away from frying pan cooking as much as possible.

What's Cooking for Breakfast? Suppose four of you are going, and all agree that in the morning such items as fruit juice, coffee, tea or chocolate, bacon or ham, eggs and toast represent a hearty breakfast, with pancakes occasionally for variety. Assume that each person will drink about 6 ounces of fruit juice, three cups of coffee, three tablespoons of sugar for three cups, and possibly three good squirts of condensed milk (unless you all drink coffee black), at least four slices of bacon or a large slice of ham, two eggs, and two pieces of toast with two pats of margarine or butter. (Precooked dry cereals for a change will also stick to your ribs!)

If these amounts are multiplied by four hunters, fishermen, etc., times 14 days (extent of this safari), the total amount will represent the amount of food needed for all breakfasts while on this particular jaunt.

Saddlebag Lunches Don't take lunch food that will spoil quickly; food poisoning can result! Processed meats not under refrigeration spoil quickly, especially if carried in a pack or saddlebag. Egg sandwiches (either fried or hardboiled), cheese, soft-spread moist peanut butter that spreads easily, jellies, jams, honey, roast beef, and steak are much safer. Sandwiches should be individually wrapped in waxed paper or put in baggies. If you desire sardines or kippered snacks, don't make sandwiches out of them at camp—do it on the trail. Soda crackers, Ry-Krisps and other kinds of dry hard bread won't be stale like regular baker's bread. If you pack bread for the first few days or so and it goes stale remember that it will make excellent toast for your meals. Some campers like to use leftover pancakes or biscuits from breakfast for sandwich breads. For drinks, a can of fruit juice or powdered types of Kool-Aid can suffice for a beverage. For dessert, candy bars or hard candy will do.

The Last Meal of the Day Items necessary for supper can be handled in the same manner as breakfast. Generally, supper is likely to be a main dish centered around meat (steak for the first night out), canned fish such as salmon or fish caught in a nearby stream, canned meats such as chicken, canned beef, dry beef, etc.; vegetables; and starchy foods such as macaroni, canned potatoes, rice, or one of the several flavored Rice-A-Roni's. In any event, food should be of the dried, smoked, canned, dehydrated, or precooked kind which will not spoil.

Camp Kitchen Gear Nested aluminum cook-kits come in 2-, 4-, 6-, and 25-man sizes. I personally like and have a nested stainless steel four-man kit that I take along on all my wilderness safaris. To this I add a three gallon water pail, but find that I like to use a new five gallon kerosene can with the top cut out and a bailing wire handle for carrying and heating water. I have discarded the coffee pot that comes with the kit and added a larger one, since it seems as though most of my friends on trips drink more coffee than the kit pot holds.

Cutting Down On Clean-up Chores Aluminum cupwear is frowned on by the dyed-in-the-wool campfire cook. These cups hold heat and burn the lips, but the contents cool too quickly. Many camp cooks use heavy duty plastic-coated throw away cups for hot and cold beverages. After each meal they can be disposed of in the campfire or, in a fixed camp, rinsed out and used again. If you use coated paper plates on top of your aluminum, enameled, or plastic plates, after the meal your washing up consists of tossing the paper plates into the campfire. That doesn't leave a lot of kitchen wear to wash except a few pots and pans and your cutlery, and you can even cut this short by purchasing plastic knives, forks, and spoons at your local supermarket.

One item usually forgotten is a plastic dishpan. None of the nesting cook kits seem large enough to use as a dishwashing vessel, and who likes to cook in a utensil used to wash greasy dishes?

The Camp Oven I believe in going as light as one can even though the pack animal will be carrying the load. Nevertheless, an iron dutch oven is a must for the experienced backcountry cook. It will bake, fry, broil, roast, and stew. Moreover, it retains an even heat. However, when I do the cooking, I also like to use a folding reflector oven.

Camp Cutlery This should consist of a sharp butcher knife, a long-handled fork, a large stirring spoon, a pancake turner, and a hot pad for lifting hot kettles and the hot lid of the dutch oven. A pair of cheap cotton gloves are handy around the campfire. Instead of a hot pad, you might use a padded patio-glove to handle hot material.

The Pressure Cooker Old timers may laugh at anyone packing along a pressure cooker. Nevertheless, I have seen many experienced pack-trippers using them in wild country. I pack a small one along for high-altitude cooking.

Since water boils at a lower temperature at high altitude, a longer cooking time is required. Many outdoorsmen forget this when they hit the high elevation trails of the Rockies and Sierra Nevada Ranges.

You must remember that the boiling point of water

drops approximately 2° Fahrenheit for each 1,000 foot increase in altitude. For instance, water at sea level will boil at 212°F; at 5,000 feet, 203°; and at 10,000 feet, 193°. At elevations up to 10,000 feet little difficulty is encountered in cooking most foods if proper precautions are taken, but above that difficulties may begin. Foods that require a considerable amount of cooking should not be taken along unless you use one of the new lightweight pressure cookers now available. Using a pressure cooker will cut cooking time down at any elevation.

Cooking Time in High Country Food prepared in an oven requires slightly higher heat in high country. For baking or roasting food to be done in the recipe's specified time, a moderate heat of 300° F will do at up to 3,000 feet. Between 3,000 and 4,000 feet increase the temperature to 350°F; at 5,000 feet increase it to 400°F, etc.

The Cooking Fire Don't forget to get a fire permit* before leaving on a safari! Check ahead of time to make sure that the area you plan on entering is not closed due to dangerous fire weather.

Over the years I have gained many pleasant memories of hundreds of cooking fires and campfires while on patrol in the high country, and I recall this little rhyme from the book *Two Little Savages*:

> First a curl of birch bark as dry as it can be,
> Then some twigs of soft wood dead from off a tree,
> Last of all some pine knots to make the kettle foam,
> And there's a fire to make you think you're sitting right at home.

* A wilderness permit is required in all wilderness and primitive areas and is a fire permit in these areas.

Be careful about where you build your campfire. A Hunter's Lay such as this must be supervised.

Choosing the Spot This is an important factor in fire safety in the woods! Don't build a fire near heavy brush fields, thick dry grass, a rotten log, or under low-lying tree limbs! If possible, build it on a flat rocky place or on a sandbar. If you have to build it in heavy woods, clear away all forest litter down to mineral soil in a ten foot circle.

The Trench Lay If you have to build a fire on a windy day, build a trench lay. In an open spot clear of all pine needles and debris, dig a trench just wide enough so that the edges will support and fit your pots, about a foot deep, and two or three feet long. Widen the windward end to catch the breeze for good draft. You can place a rock at this end to use as a draft regulator. This type of ground cooking stove doesn't require much fuel and is safer than an above the ground fireplace on a windy day.

The Rock Fireplace If you are camped where there are plenty of rocks, you can build a simple rock stove. Choose rocks of an even size and as nearly flat on top and bottom as possible. After clearing the spot down to plain dirt, arrange the rocks in two rows, close enough together to support your cooking utensils. The back end can be closed with a rock, and a rock in front can be used to act as a draft regulator.

The Hunter's Fire Lay If no suitable rocks are handy in the woods, you can make a stove similar to the rock type mentioned above by using hardwood logs two or three feet long, and about six inches apart. Since this kind of fireplace is made of wood, it should be well-dirted to retard burning, and you'll have to replace the logs from time to time.

The Keyhole Type I have seen more of this type of fireplace in hunting camps and base camps than any other kind. It is made of rocks outlined like a keyhole.

One places his pots on the narrow end for cooking and uses the larger end for a warming or campfire. **Warning!** Never leave your fire unattended at anytime! Be certain that it is OUT when you leave! You can be fined $1,000, one year in prison, or both for leaving a fire unextinguished. If your fire gets away you can be made to pay the suppression cost, and this may run into hundreds of thousands of dollars!

A Word About Dehydrated Food Thank goodness the days of the three "B's" are gone. All the old-timers had was bacon, beans, and bannock. Now the outdoorsman can choose from a wide variety of deliciously seasoned, concentrated, moisture-proof, non-perishable, lightweight foods that need no refrigeration and will keep for years.

Campsite dinners are freeze-dried for convenience on the trail.

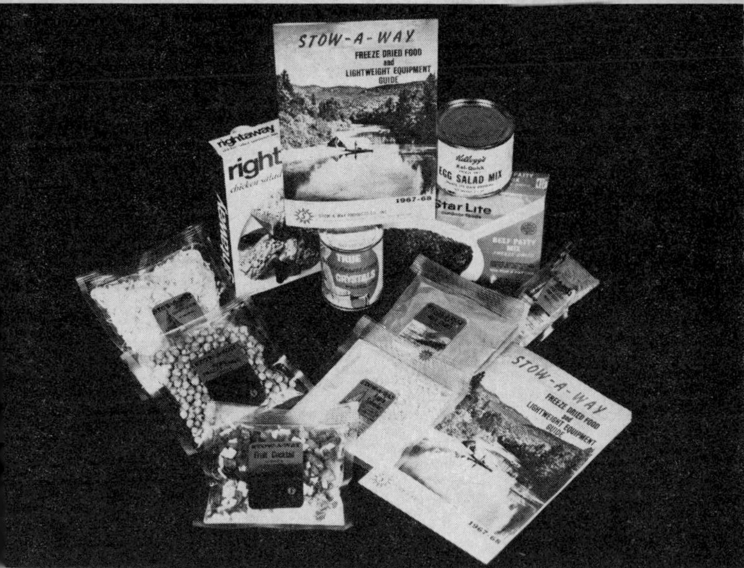

Packaged food enables you to take perishables with you on your trip. (Stow-a-Way Products)

Suit Your Taste How about a "good" hearty meal in the high country? Nothing like fresh air and exercise to build an appetite that will demand lots of camp grub. Modern methods of packaging and flavoring have been improved tenfold. But outdoor cooking with these specialty foods requires a little practice, especially if the meal is to be co-ordinated and all foods ready at the same time. Many of the foods can be combined or changed to suit your taste, and with a little imagination they can become a real gourmet meal.

Campers can discover a multitude of uses for a pack of plastic sandwich bags. Use them for carrying soap, toilet articles, film, camera, notebook, or to keep sand off your watch or billfold.

Trail Pack's "Kwik-Lunch" is especially helpful for hunters who are stalking game and don't want to take time out to cook.

SAMPLE OF BERNARD'S INDIVIDUAL KAMP-PACK ENVELOPES*

Number	*Item*	*Net Weight Ounces 4-Man Pack Double for 8-Man Pack*
1.	Apple Sauce Mix	4
2.	Mixed Fruit Sauce Mix	6
3.	Hot Biscuit Mix	10
4.	Instant Farina Cereal Complete with Milk and Sugar	6
5.	Instant Ralston Cereal Complete with Milk and Sugar	6
6.	Sweet Cream Buttermilk Pancake Mix	12
7.	Ginger Sweet Cream Buttermilk Pancake Mix	12
8.	Orange Sweet Cream Buttermilk Pancake Mix	12
9.	All Purpose French Toast Batter Mix	6
10.	Boysenberry Flavored Pancake & Waffle Syrup Mix	8
11.	Maple Flavored Pancake & Waffle Syrup Mix	8

* Bernard's Food Industries (Kamp-Pack), PO Box 487 San Jose, California 95103.

12.	Egg Omelette De Luxe	4
13.	Scrambled Eggs De Luxe	4
14.	Chicken Gumbo Soup	2½
15.	Chicken Noodle Soup	2
16.	Chicken Rice Soup	2
17.	Minestrone Soup	5½
18.	Potato Soup Supreme	8

Bernard's Food Industries markets over 100 dehydrated food items.

SAMPLE KAMP-PACK MENUS

(4-Man—12 Full Meals)
(1 man 4 days or 4 men 1 day)
(8-Man—24 Full Meals)
(1 man 8 days or 8 men 1 day)

Menu #3

Breakfast

Ginger Sweet Cream Buttermilk Pancakes
Maple Flavored Syrup
Hot Chocolate

Lunch

Spanish Rice Dinner
Hot Biscuits
Fruit Punch

Dinner

Chicken Rice Soup
Camper's Vegetable Stew
Banana Instant Stir 'N' Serve Pudding
Chocolate Milk Shake

Menu #7

Special Low Moisture Meat Item

Breakfast

Scrambled Eggs De Luxe
Hot Biscuits
Hot Chocolate

Lunch

Minestrone Dinner
Hot Biscuits
Limeade

Dinner

Potato Soup Supreme
Beef Mulligan Stew
Butterscotch Instant Stir 'N' Serve Pudding
Vanilla Milk Shake

Extras: Both menus contain Miracle Sponge and Detergent, Pure Vegetable Shortening, Salt, Hard Candies, and Toilet Tissue.

Note: See appendix for a list of other excellent sources where dehydrated foods may be obtained.

Cooking with Kamp-Pack Always read and follow carefully the simple instructions on each Kamp-Pack envelope.

Soaking When your directions say to soak the contents in water before cooking, measure the water accurately and stir in the contents of the package as soon as you reach camp. (Each Kamp-Pack envelope is marked for liquid measuring.) Stir the food occasionally as you proceed to make camp. If you can set it in a warm place to soak, do so; just be sure that it warms slowly during the soaking time. (Longer soaking improves taste.)

Making a Paste When your directions say to make

a paste of the contents, pour the dry contents into a pan or bowl and add water from the directed amount slowly, stirring steadily until the material makes a thick paste. (With most things this can be done right in the Kamp-Pack envelope.) With the back of your spoon mash out all lumps, then add more water slowly until the material will mix easily into the rest of the water.

Simmering When your Kamp-Pack food needs simmering or boiling, let it come to the bubbling point fairly slowly and then continue to cook slowly—just enough to keep the bubbles coming up. Hard boiling is not necessary or good for these foods. It helps to keep a lid on your cooking pan, but remember to watch for things that boil over and to stir things often enough so they won't stick on the bottom.

Food Storage Suggestions for Campers As a rule, campers who keep a clean camp, and use a minimum of odorous foods are less bothered by bears than those campers who do not keep a clean camp and allow garbage to collect. However, any food or food container that emits an odor is a natural target for bears. Food left on tables or in open boxes is a definite invitation to bear damage.

1. Food should not be stored on a table or in your tent.
2. Seal surplus food in clean wrapping material or in airtight containers.
3. Keep your food as cool as possible.
4. Metal chests with good locks make fair storage receptacles, although experience has shown that not all metal chests are bear-proof.
5. Campground and backcountry campers often suspend their supplies between two trees out of a bear's reach.
6. Burn all garbage and food containers, including cans, in backcountry camps.

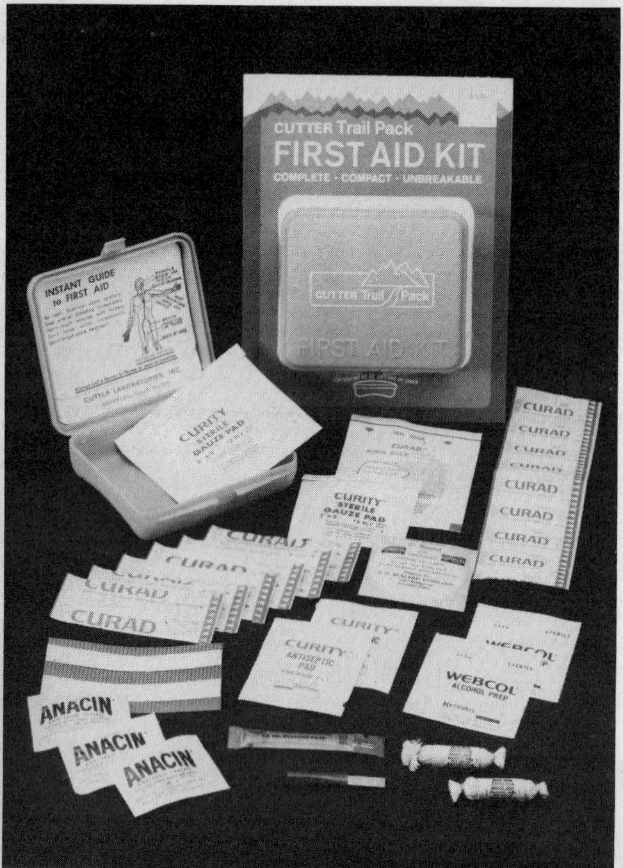

A first-aid kit is a must for traveling in the back country.

11

First Aid if You Need It!

First Aid for Man Leaders of trail riding groups and packers on extended trips far away from modern transportation and medical facilities should prepare themselves for emergencies in the backwoods by completing at least the Standard Red Cross First Aid Course. In fact, all guides, packers, and outfitters should be required to take the Advanced Course!

Who Needs It! Once in a great while something does happen in the backcountry so that first aid must be given to a member of a party. These incidents usually occur far from professional medical aid. Therefore, at times it is necessary to be a "do-it-yourself" man. With the exception of snakebite, the cardinal rule is DON'T OVERTREAT! Fortunately, most people who enter wilderness country are likely to be accident alert.

Immunization Whenever you are around stock or their pastures, or along a trail, it is important to have tetanus immunization. Be *sure* that you and all members of your party have tetanus shots before going into the mountains. Every rider should also have a typhoid immunization shot.

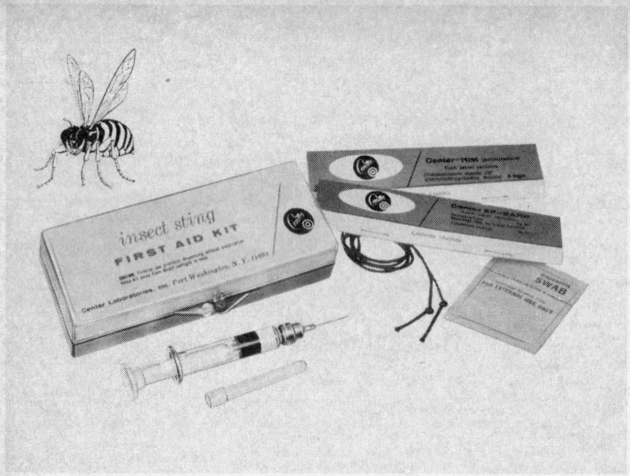

An insect sting kit is an important item, especially if anyone in your party is allergic to insect stings.

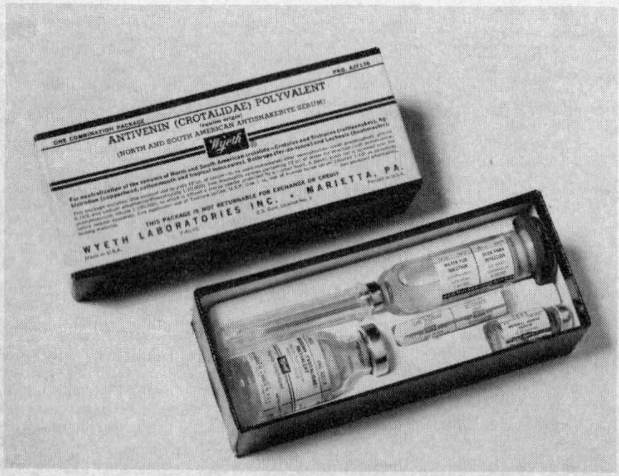

Antisnakebite serum should be included in your first aid preparations.

Dangers from Bee or Wasp Stings More people die from bee stings than from being struck by poisonous snakes, so if you are allergic to stings of this kind, be sure to have your doctor give you shots to protect you on the safari. You should also carry an anti-bee sting syringe kit with you. Keep it on your person, not in your saddlebags!

Antibiotics Many experienced riders carry antibiotics, antihistamines, and pain killers in their first aid kits when they're on extended pack trips in remote areas. Contact your doctor in advance for his recommendations on what drugs, medicines, and vitamin pills you should take along.

Respiratory Ailments Any person with a history of asthma or other respiratory ailments should get medications to take along on the trip and instructions from his doctor on how to administer them properly.

Pneumonia Pneumonia in the high country is serious and not uncommon. The victim will have a high fever and rapid breathing. He must have absolute rest, be kept warm, and receive early medical attention. It might be wise to carry some penicillin tablets in your kit!

The USFS First Aid Guide Over the years, I have found the United States Forest Service First Aid Guide to be one of the best. The Guide is small, compact, and complete, and will slip into your saddlebag, without taking up too much space.

12

First Aid for Your Mount

Wilderness Aid and Backwoods Medicine for Your Stock Like man, horses, mules, and burros are susceptible to such a multitude of ailments and injuries that a comprehensive treatise on the subject is beyond the scope of this handbook. It would require a volume too large for the horseman to carry about in his saddlebags. Consequently, only the more common injuries and diseases will be considered here.

Care of Cuts and Wounds Remember that warm blooded animals are subject to infections and blood poisoning the same as man is. Therefore, it is imperative to use as sterile a method as possible in treating an animal under field conditions in the woods. At the home ranch it is a case of knowing what to do until the vet arrives. In remote backcountry, it is a do-it-yourself job.

Prevention Lacerations are common among the equine species, and proper care is important if infection and unnecessary scars are to be avoided. Most cuts and wounds could be prevented if care were taken to eliminate sharp objects such as protruding nails, pieces of metal, glass, and loose barbed-wire in the animal's corral or stable. In the backcountry most injuries are from falls, cuts from sharp rocks and dead brush along the trail, or from a vicious kick or bite from another animal.

Wound Management The first step in wound management is to control bleeding or hemorrhage if any is present. The best way to do this is with pressure, applied either by hand or with a tight compress bandage. Once the bleeding has been controlled, the wound will heal much more rapidly if you shave the hair back from the wound for at least an inch all around. If the wound is contaminated with dirt or other debris, wash it thoroughly with soap and water, then dry and apply healing powder and bandage if possible.

Dried alum or burnt alum is sometimes employed as a dusting powder to check growth of proud-flesh and to control bleeding.

Wound Powder In my saddlebags I carry a small can of BFI antiseptic and surgical powder that has proved excellent in healing wounds for both man and beast. Another good healing powder is a small 1⅓ ounce plastic powder-puffer bottle of healing powder sold by Saddle-Mate, Hess & Clark, Ashland, Ohio 44805, also obtainable at your local vet's. Both of these powders are fine to use on wire cuts, saddle galls, rope burns, and other abrasions that are the normal part of a working animal's life.

Saddle Galls These stubborn sores are much like boils, because they often contain a core which prevents normal healing. Any healing salve or lotion will bring about a permanent cure. Mix equal parts tincture of iodine and glycerine, shake well together, and apply this to parts involved morning and night.

Rabies Bites from a rabid animal are rare out on the trail. Nevertheless, a few pack animals have been bitten by a rabid skunk, fox, or other small sick animal. This always results in death.

Struck by a Rattlesnake Animals struck by a rattlesnake generally recover. The venom kills by weight. In other words, a snake that struck an animal as large as a horse would generally cause a large swelling, and the horse would be sick for several days. A small animal would probably die from the same bite. Grazing stock are usually struck on the nose, face, or legs as they feed or travel along a trail.

Treat snakebitten animals the same way you would treat humans. Check the First Aid chapter for treatment.

Nail in Foot This is a serious accident in stock, for it may not only put the animal out of commission for a long period by causing an abscess in the foot, but it also allows the germs of lockjaw to enter the system.

Have some tincture of iodine ready in your first aid kit, so that when the nail is pulled out you can pour it in before the cavity closes. Next, clean the foot in some warm water to which a tablespoon of Lysol has been added. Crush half a dozen aspirin to a powder, mix with syrup or honey, and smear on the lower teeth of the victim to ease the pain. Apply antiseptics daily.

Cutter Tetanus Vaccine Single doses of two Cutter products, *T-Troxol*™ and *Encepholtm* are available in disposable syringes manufactured by the Cutter Laboratories, Fourth & Parker St., Berkeley, California 94710, long a leader in the veterinary drug field. They are also makers of Cutter Snakebite and Mosquito Kits.

T-Troxol provides top quality, long term immunization. The vaccine is a purified and concentrated toxoid producing durable, active immunity by stimulating a response in the animal to build its own lasting immunity, without the undesirable side effects often seen with unrefined toxoids.

Encephol provides effective protection against sleeping sickness. Stock may be immunized with either Western or Eastern-Western type *Encephol* vaccine, depending on the geographic location. Cutter is the world's largest producer of sleeping sickness vaccines.

New Horse Flu Vaccine A unique new equine influenza vaccine, containing both equine and human virus strains, has been produced by Jensen-Merrell, Inc., Kansas City, Missouri 64108. The trade name is *Equi-Flu*, and it is available nationally through veterinarians.

Colic A common misconception is that colic is a disease. It is not! Colic is a term that has come into general usage to indiscriminately describe the symptoms of abdominal pain in stock. Fortunately, mules and burros are not as susceptible to the ailment as horses since they are apt to be more cautious in their eating habits.

The symptoms can vary, depending on the severity of the pain and type of colic. True colic is defined as a pain in the stomach or intestines. Colic in other than the stomach or bowel is known as false colic. To the layman they all seem the same.

What to Watch Out For: The animal may be restless, pawing and stamping his feet, looking around at his flanks, kicking at his stomach, lying down, rolling, sweating heavily, and making numerous attempts to defecate but passing only gas or small amounts of feces. At times the pains are only intermittent. With other kinds of colic, the pain is constant and the animal may groan with pain. Breathing may be difficult because of bloat pressure in the chest and on the heart. If the sickness continues, the temperature of the animal may increase.

Each animal reacts differently, depending on the severity of the attack. The violent actions of the animal are apparent to both the tyro and experienced horseman alike. Get treatment going immediately. Get a veterinarian if possible.

Tympanitic Colic This type is sometimes called *wind colic*, and is due to the enlarging of the hollow intestines or bowels after a horse has eaten food that ferments easily. The main causes are overfeeding, watering while hot, use of feed that the animal has not yet become accustomed to, ordinary indigestion resulting from improper mastication, and systemic disorders.

Tympanitic colic can be caused by *any* food that will produce gas after being eaten, for example, cut grass rich in clover or too much green alfalfa, as well as wet or frosted green feed. Indigestible and spoiled feeds (moldy hay or grain) are also a basic cause of colic. Old dry straw is one cause of obstruction colic. Any ingestion of food too dry for an animal to digest may cause the trouble. In the backcountry, the rider should use morralys or canvas feed bags. If you do not have them, pour the grain out on a canvas manty or other canvas. Ingestion of large amounts of sand can cause trouble. Grain should never be just poured out on the ground for the animals to feed on!

In general it is best to stay away from food like green clover that is likely to ferment easily, especially if it is wet or has been frosted. Poor quality roughage is another cause. A sudden change of feed, eating when fatigued, overeating, and working a horse too soon after he has been fed may also contribute.

Spasmatic Colic The villain in this case is the accumulation of large masses of ingested material in the intestines, preventing the escape of gases arising from fermentation, and thereby causing great pressure against the intestinal organs. The pressure is responsible for the internal pains suffered.

This type of colic produces symptoms similar to those manifested in common wind colic, but more pronounced. Rolling is more vigorous and more pain is apparent, excessive sweat may appear, and in advanced stages the ears and nose become cold. Spasm pains are intermittent, with brief periods of comparative relief, and each spasm is more severe than the preceding one.

Action must be taken as soon as symptoms are recognized. Drench with a quart of warm water in which a teacup of Epsom salts have been thoroughly boiled. If favorable results are not obtained within an hour, lead the animal around slowly and prevent it from rolling on the ground. To relieve gas pressure caused by colic, some outfitters carry a can of *Turcapsol. Turcapsol* is manufactured by the Pitman Moore Company, and can be secured only by a prescription from a veterinarian. If you do not have *Turcapsol*, use a solution made up of two ounces of spirits of ammonia from your first aid kit with one pint of water as a drench. Some horsemen use a plain drench of four ounces of table salt (from the camp table) in a quart of water, and it sometimes does the trick.

Another remedy is tincture of aconite, which is given to horses in ten drop doses for the relief of colic.

Laminitis (Founder) In the majority of cases this is due to overfeeding or overwatering while an animal is very warm or tired, but it may occur as the result of hard riding over a rough trail. It attacks the forefeet, and if untreated the hooves will eventually grow out long and irregular and turn up at the toe. The soles are also affected and may protrude downward to an extent that prevents the edges of the hoof from resting on the ground.

The first symptom is intense lameness, which appears quickly. In mild cases the animal moves stiffly, taking short, rapid steps with the forefeet, with the hind legs carried well forward under the body to relieve the forefeet from the weight of the body. Usually only the forefeet are affected. The affected feet are very hot. The animal's pulse and respiration are greatly accelerated, and the temperature may reach 105°F.

Remove the front shoes from the affected feet and place the victim in a well-bedded box stall. Cover the affected feet and legs as high as the knees and hocks with several layers of burlap and keep saturated with cold water. If in a remote area place the animal in a cold stream and allow him to stand for 24 to 36 hours. In this case the shoe need not be removed. A laxative diet is indicated. Early treatment is an important factor. Cases that are not cured in four or five days are likely to develop into chronic laminitis. As soon as acute pain has diminished, moderate walking exercise each day is beneficial.

Aspirin Some horsemen administer aspirin for pain. Six tablets mashed and mixed with honey or syrup and placed on back teeth will help.

Argyrol *Argyrol* in a ten percent solution is sometimes used as an antiseptic for eye, nose, and throat infections.

Compaction (Clogged Intestines) Clogged intestines may appear at times with one of the kinds of colic. Generally, one does not have the proper medicine on hand on a trail ride, nor the knowledge for proper treatment. Nevertheless, there are a couple of ways to handle the situation. Normally the intestines are clogged at a point where the obstruction can be reached by hand, and most of the material removed.

Treatment for this condition is as follows: For safety reasons, throw a soft cotton rope around the animal's neck, catch a hind foot with the running end of the rope, and tie this foot up so that the animal cannot kick. As an extra precaution, put hobbles on the front feet too. Next, grease your hand and arm with whatever lubricant is available in camp, such as butter, margarine, lard, or cooking oil, so that the delicate membrane of the lower bowel will not be injured. Then remove as much of the material as possible with your hand. Large injections of warm soapy water nearly always turns the trick, but this operation is not usually performed on a pack trip in remote areas.

Dead Stock Any stock dying from injuries or suspected contagious disease in the backcountry must be disposed of by being burned and buried. Stock injured beyond recovery along trails, campgrounds, or near streams or water sources must be destroyed. National Park and Forest regulations state that dead animals must be hauled away from any water source and buried. If it is necessary to cremate an animal during the fire season, you must notify the district Ranger of the area for permission to burn the carcass, otherwise you will have to pack in quicklime to cover the carcass in a pit and then cover with dirt.

Cause of Stock Fatalities in Summer During the summer months there is an increase in equine deaths in mountainous regions, due to the large number of stock used, and by inexperienced riders pushing their mounts and pack animals beyond their endurance by traveling too fast over steep trails, riding too far and too high without proper rest periods when climbing, and lack of good forage each night.

Animal Check-Up! The wise person has an annual

physical examination by his family physician and usually has his dentist check his teeth at least twice a year. We are generally careful to see that our automobile gets its regular winter and spring check-up along with five to ten thousand mile inspections. However, a few ranchers and private horse owners forget or neglect their stock. As long as they appear to be all right, many of us do little to make certain that the animals are in peak condition.

Yet our pack and riding stock needs care based on regular professional examination and treatment if necessary. Spring is the time to get your working animals in tip-top shape, ready to hit the trail bright eyed, bushy tailed, and full of vigor like their master should be too!

Managed Health Program Veterinarians today offer a complete "Managed Health Program," which includes regular examinations, vaccinations, and worming. Management of your stock's health is your most important obligation and responsibility as a horse owner. Protect yourself and your animals with a spring check-up!

Check Teeth Too! Too many horse and mule owners overlook and neglect their animal's teeth, mainly, I suppose, because they are not so noticeable and are not easy to check. Nevertheless, a bad tooth or teeth can be the cause of inadequate chewing. Poor mastication can lead in turn to poor nutrition or digestive upsets. The vet will see that damaged or diseased teeth get proper attention.

Veterinarian With the vast explosion in the horse, mule, pony, and burro population in the past decade, it is fortunate that there are over 16,000 veterinarian doctors practicing their profession in 3,000 counties in the United States—not including Canada or Mexico. Colleges are turning out over 20,000 DVM's each year to meet the demand. Nevertheless, you are not likely to find an animal doctor in the remote areas of our wilderness regions unless he is on a trail ride. So it will be up to you or your packer to do the honors in case of need.

One of the Worst Enemies! Over 90 percent of all horses, mules, and burros have worms! These animals are subject to more internal parasites than any other animal.

Watch out for internal parasites or worms in the stool. They migrate through the body, penetrating intestines, entering blood and lymph systems, liver and lungs, wreaking havoc with your stock's general health. Worms cause many problems, including: dull listless appearance; dry, rough-haired coat; incomplete shedding; hard keepers; erratic appetite; and bowel disorders. Other results include anemia; colic; loss of ambition and performance; intermittent lameness and skin conditions, such as jack-sores and other ailments; lockjaw; encephalomyelitis (sleeping sickness) spread by mosquitoes; and influenza.

Contact Trouble Some diseases like strangles and influenza are spread by contact (from one horse to another) or through feed boxes, utensils, and watering troughs. That's why these diseases are common at fairgrounds, shows, race tracks, rodeos, sales stables and auctions, or even sometimes on trail rides. Outbreaks are usually sudden and severe.

Keep in Mind Something you should keep in mind is that it doesn't take a serious accident, only a small puncture wound, to disable or kill your animal. Since saddle and pack stock travel in rough terrain, they are more or less accident prone by nature. You are running a needless risk if you don't protect both yourself and mount against tetanus—man is subject to this danger, too!

Bloodworms or Strongyles There are several hundred

parasites affecting horses and mules. The most serious threat to the health and life of animals kept under the conditions found on breeding farms and in pastures is the strongyles.

There are over 50 different species of strongyles. Although not all of these have been found in any one animal, almost every animal that has not been treated at intervals for their removal harbors a number of them. The different species vary considerably in size, some being scarcely visible to the naked eye whereas others reach a length of two inches.

The larger worms (also referred to as palisade worms, bloodworms, sclerotomes, and red worms) include only three species, but those forms are the most injurious parasites of the horse and mule.

The balance of these species are the small strongyles —some 40-odd in number. In a heavily infected animal, one or more of the three species of large strongyles may be present, along with a dozen or so species of smaller strongyles.

Strongyles are found throughout the North American continent wherever horses, mules, or burros are pastured. Naturally, the degree of infection will vary according to the extent of exposure, and this in turn depends upon feeding, sanitation, season and climate, and what deworming medication the animals have received over a period of time.

A single deposit of manure from an infected animal may contain hundreds of thousands of microscopic strongyle eggs, and with the life cycle being what it is, one can understand why pastured animals are almost always infected. The eggs hatch and the larva emerge in about a week (under favorable temperature and moisture conditions). The infective larva are ingested by animals in feed and water.

Severe infections with large and small strongyles result in lack of appetite, anemia, progressive emaciation, rough hair coat, sunken eyes, digestive disturbances, a "tucked-up" appearance, colic, and a general weakened condition. Sometimes the eggs and worms can be detected in the manure of infected animals.

Navicular Disease Navicular disease is a condition causing foot lameness, and it is both common and irreversible. Therefore it must be considered one of the most serious unsoundnesses for any horse or mule.

By looking at the diagram, one can see that flexing the foot, as in bending the foot to clean it, would relax the tension of the tendon as it passes over the navicular bone. Conversely, extending the foot when weight is placed on it causes an increase in pressure on the navicular bone by the now-taunt tendon.

If the navicular bone becomes diseased, the portion of the bone that the tendon passes over loses its smooth surface of cartilage and becomes roughened. This irritates the tendon at this point and pain is produced. The disease starts insidiously and is frequently well established before lameness is noticeable.

The condition almost always occurs in the front feet, and when one foot is affected, the other eventually will be. It appears that although the animal's environment, nutrition, and the type of work he does can have a great influence upon the development of the disease, heredity can also be a factor.

Factors that seem to be most important in the development of this disease include an inherent predisposition toward weakness of the navicular bone; upright conformation of the shoulder and pastern, which results in increased shock and concussion to the navicular bone; and small contracted feet. Other causes are hard, fast travel over rough trails and roads, especially hard paved roads, and direct injury to the navicular bone, caused by puncture or other wounds to the foot.

When the disease has progressed to the point where pain occurs, the symptoms of navicular disease begin to appear. At first, one may notice only that the animal appears to move with a much shortened stride, especially when turning. When observed at rest, the animal can often be seen to point on one foot, then the other, seeking relief from the tendon pressing on the navicular bone.

As the disease progresses, the feet tend to become contracted due to disuse and, in advanced cases, the shoulder muscles can atrophy and waste away. This may lead to a possible false impression that the animal is lame in the shoulder. It is difficult for the layman to diagnose navicular disease. However, a history of contracted feet and pointing would indicate navicular disease. Your veterinarian should be able to decide. However, taking an X-ray of the navicular bone is the most conclusive proof of the existence of the disease.

A local anesthetic on the part will only give temporary relief. The condition may be arrested for varying periods of time, but generally, the condition will eventually worsen. To date, there is no cure.

Horse Bots Horse bots attack horses, mules, burros, but do not attack other classes of livestock. Although four distinct species of bots have been found in the United States and Canada, only three of these are serious pests to the horse family; namely, the common horse bot or nit fly, the throat bot or chin fly, and the nose bot or fly.

Since horse bots are found in many sections of the world, it is reasonable to surmise that they were introduced into the North American continent when the first horses were imported from Europe. The common horse bot and throat bot are now distributed throughout the country wherever horses, mules, and donkeys are found, but throat bots are much more numerous in the more arid regions of the country and at higher altitudes.

Even though the bot fly does not sting an animal, deposition of the eggs causes a tickling sensation, particularly evident in the case of the nose bot fly. Animals attacked by these pests may toss their heads in the air, strike the ground with their front feet, and rub their noses on each other or any handy object.

Infected animals may show frequent digestive upsets (and at times even colic), lowered vitality, emaciation, and a general slowing down in work or riding.

Animals should be treated for bots in the late fall or early winter, at least one month before the first killing frost, by administering one of the recommended vermifuges according to directions.

About thirty days before administering a vermifuge, the eggs of the common bot fly, which may be still clinging to the body, should be destroyed by washing the animal with warm water at 120°F, or by clipping the hair.

No Feet—No Horse! How true this old adage is! Without sound feet and foot care, a horse or mule is useless to its owner. Burros, fortunately, go barefoot. Nevertheless, their feet should be inspected occasionally for any injuries or infections and moreover, these tough little characters need to have their hooves trimmed from time to time, especially if they have been packed over rough trails.

It seems extraordinary to me how anyone can neglect an animal's feet. Horses and mules are often allowed to go for long periods of time between shoeings, stand for days on end in urine and feces-drenched stalls or in small corrals, and in extremely arid climates are left without any application of a hoof dressing so that the feet become so brittle that they crack. Many owners who are willing to groom mounts adequately are not in the habit of inspecting the animal's feet daily and cleaning them thoroughly. Any object, such as a nail, penetrating the sole of the foot may go for days undetected because of this neglect and will often cause a stubborn, deep-seated infection which is difficult to heal.

Care of the Feet The value of a horse lies chiefly in its ability to move. The important points in the care of a horse's feet are to keep them clean, prevent them from drying out, and trim them so they retain their proper shape and length. You should learn the names for the parts of a horse's foot.

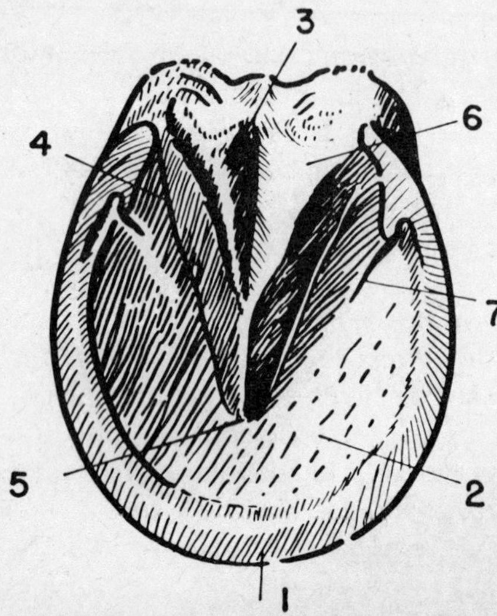

Parts of the foot of the horse: 1—Bearing edge and hoof wall. 2—Sole. 3—Median furrow of the frog. 4—Lateral furrow of the frog. 5—Apex of the frog. 6—Branch of the frog. 7—Bar.

Each day, clean the feet of horses that are shod, stabled, or used. Use a hoof-pick for cleaning. Work from the heel toward the toe, and be sure to clean out the depressions between frog and bars. While you are cleaning the feet, inspect them for loose shoes and thrush.

Thrush Thrush is a disease of the foot characterized by a pungent odor. It causes a softening of tissues in the cleft of the frog, in the junction between the frog, or in the junction between the frog and bars. This disease produces lameness and, if not treated, can be serious.

A picture of patience waiting for his master.

13

Selecting a Saddle or Packhorse—Rent or Buy?

Is a Soundness Examination Necessary? Whenever an inexperienced horseman decides to purchase a horse I suggest that he secure the services of a veterinarian to assist him in making a choice of a healthy animal. To put things in their proper perspective, you must remember that this judgment of soundness for which you ask the veterinarian is an opinion only and subject to many variables. The horse or mule as a biological entity is subject to continuous change. Don't blame your veterinarian if something happens to your animal(s) the day after your purchase. Disease may come overnight, unexpected death may happen a day or so later due, let us say, to a weakened blood vessel rupturing. This or any other injuries may not be apparent the day the animal was examined. Human beings are subject to the same uncertainty.

The animal may have a mild arthritic condition that may not show up clearly except at certain times, such as just before he is warmed up or the day after a hard ride, and, due to clever timing of the former owner, this may go unnoticed at the time of the examination. The animal may have been treated with drugs to alleviate the symptoms of an underlying disease or condition and this also may go unnoticed at the time of examination. The examining veterinarian can judge only what he sees at the moment.

Often a buyer is put at a disadvantage involving some saddle horse or mule at an auction. Here the buyer has no chance to examine the animal(s) before purchase and the seller wanting to get rid of a certain animal may have "doctored" his animal before it is sold. Not many auctions will condone these practices if they are observed. Nevertheless, it is possible for an unscrupulous owner to tranquilize a vicious animal or cover up lameness by using a local anesthetic. Here is where that old adage: "Buyer beware . . . it is a seller's market!" comes in.

Try Out if Possible When considering a potential riding or pack animal for purchase, it would be smart to request a trial period of at least several days of riding or packing before having a veterinarian check the animal over. This trial period will hopefully allow time for any deviation of temperament or unsoundness of wind or limb to make themselves apparent.

Naturally, this is not always possible. The owner of an animal in first class condition may think twice before handing over his steed to a rider of unknown riding and handling abilities for a trial period, being apprehensive of what might happen to the animal's training or of a possible lawsuit if the prospective buyer is injured in the meantime by the animal. The trial period is a point to be negotiated, and is very important, especially if the animal is completely unknown to the prospective buyer.

During a soundness examination, some veterinarians are asked questions on conformation, breeding, temperament, suitability, and schooling. Remember, this is *not* an area of veterinary medicine, and that it takes many years of experience and study in these areas to qualify as an expert and to be an expert on one breed. It is not proper to ask a veterinarian questions that properly should be put to an expert in these particular fields. It is the place of the expert horseman to pass on such matters as the fine points of conformation and schooling.

Look Them Over Carefully! Occasionally a Standardbred or American Saddlebred horse is seen being ridden along a mountain trail. Nevertheless the Saddlebred has too high an action and is too excitable to endure hard trail usage. The Standardbred's action is often too rough and jolting for trail riding.

Personally, I prefer my Morgan and half-Morgan saddle and pack animals for my occasional safari into the high country.

Range Horses Some range horses (sometimes called Mustangs) compete well with Thoroughbreds, which are rarely shorter than 14 hands. A 14-hand horse may stand up well under trail conditions better than one 17 hands or vice-versa. Weight itself does not have much to do with making a good trail horse. Even a 900-pound horse in good physical condition may hold its own with an equally fit animal weighing 1,100 to 1,200 pounds.

Characteristics Certain characteristics, however, are of great importance. Any saddle or pack animal, regardless of breed, that is mountain trail broken and classified as an "easy keeper" generally makes a good trail animal.

The Easy Keeper An easy keeper is a horse or mule that can do a lot of trail mileage on little forage. Generally, whatever breed he is, the animal must have a short back with close coupling; that is, the distance between the withers and the point of the croup should be short, and the space between the end of the ribs and the point of the hip should be as narrow as possible. The ribs should be well-sprung, round, and set well back; the chest broad and powerful; and the brisket wide. The underline should be clean, strong-looking and well muscled, and the throat should be straight and not fleshy. All these characteristics generally point to a powerful and usually courageous animal with great lung capacity, a strong heart, and much endurance.

Should You Rent or Buy? The prospective owner should look for the following characteristics if he is purchasing or renting an animal for his personal use or for a member of his family, and wants the best.

USFS Specifications. The animal should be between five and eight years old, since he will reach his full growth between four and five years; he should be alert, gentle, and well-broken. He should neck-rein readily, and stand quietly when tied to rail or post or when tie-rope or reins are grounded. He should be between 14 and 16 hands high (one hand equals four inches) and weigh between 950 and 1,150 pounds. His head should be medium size, broad between the eyes, and the line from poll to muzzle straight, with nostrils widely expanded. The eyes should be clear, bright, and full. The ears should be pointed, active, alert, and well apart.

The neck should be strong and swell smoothly to the shoulders with crest arched. The windpipe should stand out large. The chest should be deep and the floor should be close coupled to hips, full and deep. The animal's back should be well-muscled, smooth, short, and only

Owning your own horse can be a do-it-yourself business, if you take the trouble to learn how to do it right. (U.S. Forest Service photo.)

slightly curved. Its withers should be well-formed, and not too thick. The hips should be wide and level, well muscled, and smooth. His croup length and width should be well proportioned. The thighs should be long, muscular, and well-spread. Hocks, of course, should be straight, broad in front, and sharp behind. Front legs should be flat and well-corded or muscular. They should be long from elbow to knee, and short from knee to ground, with straight lines side and front. The knee should be broad and deep; the cannon short, flat, and clean appearing. The pastern should be properly proportioned and slope 45 to 50 degrees, and should be strong and elastic.

Judge the animal's actions as he is being ridden about, and then mount him yourself and put him through his paces. Notice if he rides smoothly and appears to be well-balanced; that his legs unfold gradually and steadily, that his knee action is easy, and hock movement smooth and springy; that his step is light, measured, very deliberate and sure. His feet should be lifted clear of the ground, and placed down evenly with an elastic movement. His legs should be thrown well forward in stride. His head should be carried well up and not with a jerky motion. An animal in good health will have a gloss to his hair, with smooth skin.

Selecting a Pack Horse In general, a pack horse should be between 15 and 15½ hands in height, and weigh from 1,000 to 1,150 pounds. He should be compact and stocky in build, with medium withers, straight well-muscled back, deep girth, straight, large-boned legs, and good feet. He should also be broken to ride. Types of horses that cause trouble as pack animals are those with withers that are too thick, too flat, or too thin; back too short, too long, sway-backed, or roached; broad-ribbed, draft type of chest; and those with an excessively large barrel.

In addition to desirable conformation, pack horses should be gentle and free of vicious habits, and should walk, trot, and gallop freely and boldly when used as riding mounts in emergency. There should be little motion to the back at the walk, and its action should be low at the trot. There must not be excessive transverse motion (side swaying) of the body in the rear of the forequarters at the walk, nor excessive up and down movement of the saddle position at the trot.

Some pack animals are too sway-backed or have too high withers and consequently require more padding than an animal that is called a hogback. Some barrel-shaped stock are difficult to pack, and if you do have to pack one of these, the pack should be slung low and no top pack used.

Cinch Area The cinch area of pack animals varies considerably. If the animal is "potbellied," the cinches aren't too hard to keep in their proper place. On a thin-bellied animal, I always connect the center of the double-rigged riding or pack saddle cinches together with a piece of latigo leather or with a piece of leather thong. This prevents the rear cinch from slipping too far backward.

The Purchaser The purchaser of a saddle pack horse should, when possible, exercise the greatest deliberation in inspection of the animal he proposes to buy. Of course, it is true that a saddle animal which may suit one man may not suit another, but the suggestions which follow will assist the inexperienced buyer in selecting a fairly satisfactory animal for use, until such time as his own experience may tell him that an animal of other qualities will suit his individual likes better.

The prospective purchaser should always make a personal inspection of the animal he is considering, this rule holding good in every case unless he can secure advice from some person whom he knows to be absolutely reliable. Professional horse dealers and other persons having horses for sale usually will not or else cannot give the buyer complete details concerning the animal negotiated for. As a result of this, the buyer may eventually discover characteristics in an animal that were not apparent, or were not made known to him, before or at the time the purchase was made.

Age Under ordinary circumstances a horse should be in his prime at from seven to ten years of age. As a matter of fact, however, most pack or saddle animals are not given proper attention, and as a result may be of little value after they reach the age of seven or eight. At any rate, if the buyer has reason to believe that he may want to sell the animal within a year or so, and wants to secure no less than the purchase price, he should not purchase an animal older than eight, unless there is every indication that the animal is perfectly sound. Even then, in view of the fact that there is little demand for horses exceeding eight or ten years of age, there is always a question of being able to dispose of them on short notice.

Size A horse weighing from 900 to 1,000 pounds is sufficiently heavy for all ordinary field work. Larger ones do not possess the capacity for continued climbing, traveling over rough country, or subsisting on short rations that smaller animals do. They may prove satisfactory for level traveling over good roads, but cannot be recommended for mountain travel.

Build The most efficient type of saddle animal for mountain work has a short back, is high at the withers and deep from there to the chest, which is full and very broad; the legs are moderately short and are straight and strong with compact joints and sound hoofs; the head is wide between the eyes and also between the ears and is carried well up, but not high, when traveling; the nose is slightly Roman; and the eyes are large and clear and show very little of the white.

Color Only three colors, with their variations, actually affect the efficiency of a saddle animal. These are white, what is known as "pinto," and "buckskin." The first usually indicates inbreeding, and when this is present the animal, of course, suffers from constitutional weakness in one or more forms. This color is not to be confused with the cream color of a distinct breed of horses noted for their great intelligence.

Pinto horses (which may also be known as "paint,"

A good horse is worth whatever you have to pay for him. (U.S. Forest Service photo.)

"speckled," "piebald," or "calico") are descendants of the Indian pony and are very hardy and strong, but seldom attain great size.

Buckskin (also called "dun" or "claybank") horses have dark stripes around the legs above and below the knees and hock joints and another extending the entire length of the spinal column. They are descendants of a distinct breed of Spanish ponies noted for their great powers of endurance. They are the toughest and hardiest horses that can be obtained, are intelligent and usually docile unless ill-treated, and are seldom vicious.

Black horses may suffer more from heat than other colors, bays may be the most vicious, and chestnuts may have the tenderest skins, but actual experience in the field has failed to prove or disprove any of these theories.

General Disposition Many horses resent having their ears grasped when the halter or bridle is to be adjusted or removed. They object to being slapped on the side or flank, do not like to be rubbed or curried, pull back or kick at the stall or other animals when tied, and acquire many unpleasant habits of a similar nature. Their examination in this respect should be very thorough, and when such tendencies are shown it should constitute a valid reason for rejection of the animal. The common idea that such animals should be purchased merely because they may be secured for less money is a mistake that should never be made. Animals having as few faults as possible will still prove enough of a problem for the beginner in horsemanship.

Eyes A blind or partially blind horse is practically worthless for saddle use, and should never be secured for such work. The defect is often difficult to detect by casual observation of the animal's eyes, and the examination in this respect cannot be too thorough. A very satisfactory method of doing this is to take the animal from the stable into strong sunlight. If the lids or pupils shrink the sight is defective or at least weak: the change of light should not cause any discomfort.

Another means of determining defective eyesight is to pass the hand quickly across an animal's line of vision and close to the eyes. When this is done and no apparent notice of it is taken by the animal, the eyes are wholly or partially sightless.

A good, strong, sound eye is clear, the ball glistens, has a regular contour, and is not spotted or blotched. The white should be clear in color with only the faintest trace of minute thread-like blood vessels showing beneath the surface. Excessive lachrymal secretions indicate an injured eye and should be carefully investigated. A "glass" eye is not necessarily weak, but its presence always lessens the market value of an animal. In old horses the eyeball is distinctly sunken in the socket.

Pulse Normal heart action is approximately as follows:

Colt, two to four weeks old
70 to 90 beats per minute
Colt, six to twelve months
45 to 60 beats per minute
Colt, two to three years
40 to 50 beats per minute
Mare . . . . 35 to 40 beats per minute
Gelding . . . . 33 to 38 beats per minute
Stallion . . . . 28 to 32 beats per minute

Check the pulse by placing your ear against the animal's left side just in back of the elbow joint. A dull, regular, thudding sound indicates a healthy heart, while

Note the fine, intelligent head of this Mountie's horse. (Photo courtesy of Canadian Government Travel Bureau.)

wheezing, roaring, rattling, or irregular sounds indicate the opposite.

Another method of checking the pulse is to place your fingers up under and between the lower jaws immediately behind the flat cheek muscles. If the pulse is not located at once move your fingers forward or backward until the right spot has been reached.

Respiration This should be regular and without severe muscular effort, and in a healthy animal occurs at the approximate rate of one breath to every three beats of the heart. Unless the respiratory system is impaired the breaths are inaudible except at very close range.

Many animals suffering from improper respiration develop symptoms when strenuously exercised that are not apparent during inactivity. For this reason it is always well to give them ten or fifteen minutes of lively exercise before the purchase is made.

Hearing If an animal is spoken to sharply at a time when it happens to be looking away from you, it will indicate that it hears you by a sudden twitch of the ears or head in your direction. If no such action results the animal's hearing is probably impaired.

Legs The distance from the body between the forelegs and the ground should be about the same as that from the withers to the body at the same point. The legs should set well apart at the breast, be straight at the hock joints, and the portions above these joints should be full and well muscled. None of the joints in the legs should buckle in any direction, bear any unnatural enlargements, or appear stiff.

Hooves Sound hooves have straight, symmetrical walls, broad heels, a full frog, and a generally oily appearance. Flaring, bell-shaped, cracked, or otherwise disfigured hooves should be disqualifying factors. They mean trouble for both animal and prospective buyer!

A ranger and his horse at work leading a pack string near Silver Pass in the John Muir Wilderness area. (U.S. Forest Service photo.)

14

The Care and Feeding of Horses and Mules— The Correct Way!

Caring for Your Own Stock Horses and mules are not naturally incorrigible, but such characteristics may develop as the result of improper training or treatment, and continual nagging or annoying an animal is a practice that cannot be too strongly condemned. There is a wide-spread idea that horses, mules, and burros can neither think nor reason, but men who have spent years working with or about them will invariably dispute this theory—this old Ranger included!

Watering and Feeding Horses, mules, and burros can exist on wonderfully short rations for a short period, but it is imperative that they have a certain amount of water. However, they should not be allowed free access to it while extremely warm or fatigued, nor should they be given water immediately after being fed, as in this case the water will carry the grain or forage directly into the intestines before stomach digestion has been completed. The invariable result of this is a more or less severe case of colic. The best time to water a tired or heated saddle or pack animal is after it has been allowed to rest half an hour or more. Stagnant or polluted water should never be given! Mules are better suited in some areas for packing and require less food than horses.

The Coffee Can Measurer Equine nutritive requirements are very similar to our own needs. Horses and mules need carbohydrates, fats, proteins, vitamins and minerals, and plenty of clean pure water.

Too many horse owners make the mistake of using a three pound coffee can when measuring out a grain feed for their animals. There is just too much variance: for instance, rolled barley, bran, and other equine delicacies all have a different weight. Two flakes of hay and six pounds of oats measured with a three pound coffee can is just not enough feed for the average animal.

Few horse owners know that a horse's stomach is small compared to other livestock animals, having a capacity of from eight to seventeen quarts. As a result, horses and mules should be fed three times a day, or at least morning and night. If an animal is given too much feed at one time, it will not be digested properly and the loss of nutrients not only becomes costly, but may cause an animal to founder.

An experienced horse owner will provide fresh water at all times, except after hard riding. If a hot, sweating horse were allowed to quench his thirst at once, the result could be colic. Cool him slowly instead by walking him. Allow the animal only small amounts of water until his excessive sweating and heavy breathing subside.

Horses and mules have no gall bladder, so bile is secreted by the small intestine, while the large intestine is responsible for the horse's ability to subsist on hay or grass. Moreover, it takes a good deal of range pasturage roughage to match the nutritional value of grain or commercial concentrates. Except for water, from eight to twelve gallons a day, most of the horse's diet should be made up of energy-supplying carbohydrates and fats.

Poor Practice One fault of the new or inexperienced owner is feeding by volume alone. This is a poor practice.

Because of the nature of the horse's digestive system, it generally requires bulk, a volume-weight relationship, one might say. A quart of oats weighs about one pound, while a quart of corn weighs in the neighborhood of 1.75 pounds, so oats are bulkier than corn.

Virtually all manufacturers of commercial livestock feeds publish bulletins and pamphlets suggesting rations for horses. These may be obtained free by writing to the company involved.

Present-day horsemen are much in favor of complete, all-pelleted rations in which hay and grain are combined. Pelleting prevents horses from selectively refusing ingredients likely to be high in certain dietary essentials: each bite is a balanced feed. Pelleting also prevents waste.

Scientists at the Purina Horse Research Center suggest that horses be fed at the same time each day if at all possible and that feeding programs be changed gradually. A change must take several days or more to avoid upsetting the animal's digestive system. It is when the valley owner takes his soft, fat, grass-fed mount up into the high country to graze on mountain pasturage that he gets his animal into trouble feedwise!

Health and Condition The health and condition of a horse depends largely upon the kind of food received and the hours of feeding. Feeding to obtain the best results requires a knowledge of the digestive system of animals, the food elements required for their sustenance, the correct proportions of these elements, the proper methods of preparation, and the best hours of feeding.

The Digestive System The organs of the digestive system form the alimentary canal and consist of the mouth, pharynx, esophagus, stomach, small intestines, and large intestines, consisting of the caecum, large colon, small colon, rectum, and anus. The large glands, such as the salivary glands, liver, and pancreas, are accessory organs.

The stomach is the principal organ of digestion. Its capacity is from three to four gallons. The intestines are also organs of digestion, and have a much greater capacity than the stomach.

Food is taken into the mouth and masticated. It passes through the pharynx and esophagus into the stomach, where it is partially digested and prepared for complete digestion in the intestines. Digestion is completed and the nutriment and moisture extracted in the intestines. The residue is discharged through the anus as dung.

The time required for stomach digestion varies with the class of food. Grain requires approximately twice as long as hay. For this reason hay should precede the grain ration, or else follow it by an hour or two. The latter is best when a large hay feed is given, as in the evening. A small feed of loose hay shortly before the grain takes the edge off the horse's appetite and keeps him from bolting the grain. It greatly stimulates the saliva and stomach secretions and is an aid in digestion as it furnishes the bulk necessary for proper stomach digestion.

Water remains in the stomach for only a short time,

passing quickly into the intestines, where it is collected in a part of the large intestines called the caecum. If water is given too soon after feeding, it flushes a considerable portion of the food from the stomach into the intestine before it is digested. In general, watering should be done before feeding or not until an hour or two afterward. Animals drink very little or none if watered very early in the morning, and for this reason the morning water is best given shortly before the work period or trail ride.

Food Constituents Food constituents are classified according to the function they perform in the animal system as follows:

1. Flesh making: such as linseed meal, oats, peas, beans, bran, etc.
2. Fat, heat, and energy producing: such as corn, hay, oats, etc.
3. Bone making: such as grass, hay, bran, bonemeal, milk, etc.
4. Bulk supplying, necessary to digestion (fibrous and woody material): such as hay, grass, bran, etc.
5. Watery: such as carrots, potatoes, green grass, etc.

There is no one food containing all of the required constituents, so two or more must be combined to obtain the desired ration. Natural grasses come nearer to serving this purpose than any other food.

Proportions of Various Food Components in a Ration The components of any ration depend upon the class and condition of the animals, the work required of them, the variety of available foods, the kind of shelter afforded, the climate, the season, etc. The food must be selected in such proportions as to form a balanced ration, and must be fed in such quantities at such hours as to enable the animal to obtain the greatest possible amount of nutrition from them.

Oats Oats are the safest of all grains for animals. All other grains are regarded as substitutes. Oats may be safely fed in quantities of up to 16 pounds per day, provided the animal is performing heavy work. However, because of the small size of their stomachs, animals should be fed no more than 4½ pounds at one feeding. Horses and mules should be given no more than 6 pounds daily when rested for any length of time.

Corn Corn is less a desirable feed than oats by reason of its tendency to produce heat and fat. It is best fed during the colder months of the year and combined with oats and hay.

Corn should, when practicable, be fed on the cob. One feed consists of from six to twelve ears, depending on the size of the ears, the amount of work performed. and the individual animal. When feeding shelled corn is necessary, mix with dry bran or oats, or both, to prevent bolting.

A change from oats to corn should be made gradually, substituting about two pounds of corn for two pounds of oats each successive week.

Barley Barley is a very good food for horses, and may be safely substituted for oats and fed in the same quantities. The change from oats to barley should be gradual and extend over a period of at least two weeks.

Barley may be fed whole, but due to its excessive hardness it is usually crushed or soaked in water for two or three hours before feeding.

Rye Rye is not regarded as a good forage. Should its use become necessary, it should be fed in small amounts and mixed with other feed such as oats or bran. Whenever possible, rye should be rolled or crushed before feeding. In an emergency it may be mixed, in amounts of six to ten pounds, with some bulkier grain such as bran or oats.

Wheat Wheat alone is not a safe food for horses. Only one or two pounds should be fed at first and the amount gradually increased to a maximum of six pounds a day. Wheat should be combined with some bulky grain or mixed with chaff or chopped hay. It is desirable to roll wheat before feeding.

Rice Rough rice, when rolled, crushed, or coarsely ground, may be fed in quantities up to about half of the grain ration. In an emergency it may be fed in quantities of up to 14 pounds daily.

Linseed Meal Linseed meal is an excellent food for animals that are in a run-down condition. Its effect is slightly laxative and its use will improve the gloss of the coat, so it is a useful feed during the spring shedding. As linseed meal is unpalatable to most horses, it should be mixed with other feed, such as oats and bran. As a general rule, it should not be fed in larger amounts than one-half pound daily. Smaller amounts, such as a heaping mess-kit spoonful three times a day mixed with grain, are often sufficient.

Bran Bran is an excellent food for animals. As an adjunct to a ration consisting largely of grain, it is most useful because of its mild, laxative effect. It helps in building bone and muscle without tending to fatten and adds to the general tone and condition of animals.

If dry bran is fed daily, about two pounds mixed with oats or other grain is the proper amount. Feeding bran produces more thorough mastication of the grain, adds bulk to the grain ration, and supplies slightly laxative and tonic properties. The quantities should be reduced when animals are grazed or fed alfalfa or other foods that have a laxative action.

An occasional feed of bran in the form of a mash is relished by most horses and it is quite beneficial. In this form bran has a more pronounced laxative action. Bran mashes are best given the night before a day of idleness or light exercise.

A bran mash is made by placing two or three pounds of bran in a feed pan, sprinkling a mess-kit spoonful of salt over the top, and then adding boiling water, stirring until the mixture is well-dampened but not sloppy. Cover or wrap the container in a horse cover and allow it to stand until cool enough not to burn the mouth.

Salt Horses show great fondness for salt and thrive when regularly supplied with it. It should always be available in the form of cake or rock salt placed in or conveniently near the manger. Feed pans for grain should not be used as salt containers. Under field conditions animals should be given salt about twice a week in the form of one heaping mess-kit spoonful of rock salt mixed with the grain in the feed bag.

Hay Hay cannot be wholly dispensed with for any considerable time unless it is replaced by a similar feed, such as straw, as bulk is necessary for proper digestion. Oat straw is the best substitute for hay, and the use of barley or rye straw is not recommended. Under field conditions, when issues of hay are diminished or entirely suspended, it is important that animals be grazed or fed such roughage as can be gathered.

All classes of hay, with the exception of alfalfa, are of practically equal feeding value.

Clover hay makes a good forage for draft animals. It has a laxative effect and when fed alone may make animals "washy." Clover frequently appears mixed with timothy, and when it does not comprise over 50 percent of the mixture it is an excellent hay for general use.

Alfalfa is quite laxative in its effect on animals unaccustomed to its use. Alfalfa is more like the grains than like other hays in feeding properties, and combines especially well with a grain ration of corn. The change to a ration containing alfalfa should be made gradually, beginning with two or three pounds daily. Alfalfa should not comprise much more than one-half of the hay allowance.

Pastures Good pasturage is the cornerstone of successful horse production. Great horse-breeding centers are characterized by luxuriant pastures produced on fertile soils. In season, there is no finer forage for horses.

A temporary pasture grown in a regular crop rotation is preferable to a permanent pasture that may be parasite infested.

Since horses are less likely to bloat than cattle or sheep, legume pastures are excellent for them. Specific grass or grass-legume mixtures vary widely from one area to another, according to differences in soil, temperature, rainfall, and other natural factors. Ask your county agricultural agent for pasture recommendations suitable to your locality.

Horse pastures should be well drained. Shade, water, and minerals always should be available. Pits, stumps, poles, tanks, and places dangerous to horses should be guarded.

Two fine pack horses with special pack rigging for transporting. (U.S. Forest Service photo.)

15

Miscellaneous Tips for New Horsemen

Figuring It Out! Before the outfit leaves the home corral, the packer makes sure that the "dude" has planned properly and brought enough provisions along to last the trip. Most outfitters mail a ration list to each client. This is usually a time-tried list of how much and what kinds of food and supplies are needed for a known number of people (including the packer and his helpers, such as wranglers, guides, cooks, etc.), for the specified number of days that the safari will take. Many outfitters figure that for the usual 10 to 14 day trip or more, it will take about a horse and a half per person to pack food, shelter, bedrolls, and other personal gear. That means if there are 10 people in the party, 15 pack animals will be needed, plus a saddlehorse for all members; making a total of 25 head of stock. I recommend taking an extra horse or two in case of a lost or injured animal. It does happen now and then!

Overloading Saddlebags A saddlebag rides right over your horse's kidneys. Most beginning riders overload these bags, which are only meant for a few lightweight articles. Most horsemen carry their lunch, a small first aid kit, camera, smoking material, etc. Perhaps that is why so many outfitters do not furnish saddlebags. Packed too heavily, they have caused kidney sores which are difficult to heal. Remember, it is the horse that hurts, not you, so pack your saddlebags light. Balance your riding saddle with your rifle on one side and your riata and canteen on the opposite side.

The Pack Must Be Comfortable A pack animal must be packed so that the dead-weight load is made as comfortable as possible. The burden should be carried on the top of the sides of the animal's rib-cage, not too far back and not too far forward, or you'll hamper its action. If you pack the cargo too high, you won't travel far before it begins to slip; if the cargo is packed too low, it will squeeze the horse's lower ribs and impede his breathing.

What Kind of Pack Container Is Best? Pack boxes (whether they are made of wood, plastic, leather, canvas, or fiberboard) are called either panniers, kyacks or pack bags, depending on the region where they are used. They are sometimes even called *alforja*, meaning saddlebag in Spanish. It's a matter of choice. Personally, I like the canvas type in which I can fit two empty five gallon cans that have had their tops cut out. When packed properly, this keeps breakage down on fragile items.

How to Sit in the Saddle A horse or riding mule handles itself with its front quarters. Its hind quarters are the propelling unit. A rider can help his mount by leaning slightly forward, by not leaning too far backwards, and by making the proper use of his stirrups. You no doubt have noticed the bad rider who sits back against the cantle no matter what gait the horse is using, and rides up hill and down grade with all the body weight on the animal's kidneys. As if that isn't enough, these riders sit from one side of the saddle to the other, and it appears that all they use their stirrups for is to mount and dismount. No wonder a large swelling appears on their horse's back! Riding in this manner has the same crippling action as a top heavy pack too far back on the poor animal's back. If your pack is too high and too far to the rear, the pack will weave and sway too much, and rub wear on the animal's back and kidneys as he walks along. This kind of treatment can put your stock out of action for a long time.

A Secure Pack Will Help Sooner or later a pack string will run into bee trouble. Every summer that I was on patrol in the high country, my saddlehorse, my packhorse, and I were ambushed by yellowjackets when their nest was inadvertently kicked up along the trail, or by wild bees that a bear had stirred up nearby while robbing their nest of honey. How they can sting! They keep up their attack for a long distance down the trail with the ponies bucking and squealing and scattering in all directions, attempting to avoid the hot stingers! At times there just isn't any way to avoid these mishaps. It's just part of the wilderness game.

If you haven't saddled and packed your kyacks properly and secured them with a good tight Diamond hitch, you may find eggs, sugar, coffee, oatmeal, cornmeal, and other food items all mixed up in one heck of a mess. Even if you have packed properly, the pack may get slammed into a rock bank in a narrow section of trail, or the pack animal may attempt to pass between two trees that are too close together. I have even had my pack mule lie down and attempt to roll over, and most packers have had this happen at times. If this does ever happen to you and there has been much damage to your pack, you have three choices; either give up the trip, return to the home corral and stock up again, or salvage what you can and take it from there!

Packaged Food Items All packaged food that comes in cardboard containers such as cornmeal, oatmeal, rice, flour, etc., should be placed in separate canvas or muslin bags to insure that the contents will not become mixed with other items in case of accident. I have purchased several rubberized waterproof bags of various sizes from an Army surplus store and have marked on each bag what goes in it. It only takes a moment to pick out the bags needed for any particular meal.

Waxed and Plastic Bags Waxed and small plastic bags come in handy too, for storage of toilet articles, wet face cloths, toilet soap and other small articles, and the waxed paper bags keep lunch sandwiches fresher and the contents from becoming contaminated from trail dust. When you are through with the paper bags, they make excellent campfire starters.

Packing Eggs I pack eggs by cracking them in a bowl and pouring the whole eggs into a quart jar. When I am ready to cook them, I just pour the right number of whole eggs for the meal into the frying pan. I find that powdered or dehydrated eggs can be made more tasty by adding sugar and salt to taste. Mix these eggs with powdered or canned milk, whip, place in a double-kettle, and let the boiling water in the bottom kettle do the cooking. Keep stirring until they are thick enough. The eggs will be light-colored, tasty, and a lot easier on a weak stomach than would fried or hardboiled eggs. I sometimes add a pinch of onion and sweet bell pepper flakes to add more zest to the eggs. Another way to pack eggs is to wrap each egg in a piece of paper and stuff them into a two-pound coffee can. I have carried them this way over many miles of rough trails. Some packers place the eggs in cans and place oatmeal around them, carrying two articles in one package.

Cooking Oils and Lard Butter, lard, and cooking oils should be packed tightly in cans. Bottled oil should be wrapped in several thicknesses of paper and placed upright in the box kyack.

Fresh Meat Fresh meat for the first night out should be wrapped in waxed paper, then in newspapers, and placed in the pannier where it is insulated against the hot rays of the sun.

Packing Canned Goods An easy way to pack canned goods is to take about five ordinary cans, lay them end to end on a gunny-sack laid out flat, fold back the surplus slack at the ends of the sack, roll up tight, and tie. Pack these rolls of cans horizontally in the panniers with the heaviest cans on the bottom. If all canned goods are packed this way, they will not bang around loosely and fray the pack animal's nerves. Gunny-sacks have many uses: they can be used as hobbles, morralies, tent-door mats, emergency cinches, and even as saddle blankets in a pinch.

Lanterns and Fuel Gasoline, kerosene, and lantern or stove fuels should be packed in leak-proof safety cans. Some packers use glass bottles, but there is a chance of breakage even if the bottles are wrapped well in paper and stood upright in wooden box type kyacks. All fuel, soap, detergents, etc., should be packed away from food.

Lanterns should be packed in cartons wrapped snugly and firmly with newspapers and stood upright in a wooden kyack. I pack my personal lantern in a plywood box container. Inside the box is a lantern-wrench, extra mantles, a lantern generator, and a gas strainer—just in case! I pack a couple of extra flashlight bulbs and batteries in the same box.

Other Breakable Items Small battery operated radios,

cameras, etc., not carried on your person or in the saddlebags should be bundled up in the center of the panniers with soft cargo around them.

Mark the Kyacks Number or letter your kyacks so that when you arrive at your mountain camp you will know which box the grub is in and which contains hobbles, extra halters, grazing bells, picket-pins, and horseshoe nails, along with the farrier's outfit. All these items should be packed in one special kyack. (I hope that you insulate and muffle the bell clappers on the grazing bells and any other item that would rattle and bang and cause a pack animal to spook!)

Procedure for Arriving in Camp The animals and all of you are hungry and the cook is in a hurry to get a meal going, so unpack the kitchen gear and food panniers first, and the tents, bed rolls, and rest of the gear last.

As each animal is unpacked, he should be led off and tied to a stout tree or hitch rack, far enough away from camp to keep droppings from attracting flies. Put his pack saddle, pad, and blanket near where you plan on locating the tack tent and gear, with the blanket and pad spread out flat on top of the saddle to air and dry, with the lash, lead rope, etc., and a pack cover over all. Halters may be placed with this gear or left on the animal.

The Tack Tent Many outfitters pitch a small tent in which to store the riding and packhorse gear that goes with them. A small tent doesn't weigh much and is a labor-saving piece of equipment that will pay off in wet or inclement weather, especially when it snows. Salt eating animals such as deer, porcupine, and field mice aren't so apt to chew up the gear if the tent has a zippered doorway and sewed-in floor. I have used a tent of this type for many years—after I found a timber-rattle-

A peaceful, well-planned trail camp. (U.S. Forest Service photo.)

snake inside a tent that didn't have a sewed-in floor. Snakes like to hunt for mice and other small rodents!

The Thoughtless Packer I have seen a few thoughtless would-be packers, who wouldn't think of treating a piece of machinery badly, overload their pack string and trot the laden animals along, up and down steep mountain trails in rugged terrain, never giving them a breather on steep grades. They never stop long enough when crossing a stream to let the animals wet their dry throats, and never straighten a slipped or lopsided pack or tighten a loosened cinch. On reaching camp, these same characters keep the animals tied to a tree until dark, some with packs still on! Next morning, before the stock has had sufficient time to graze, they slap on their oversized packs and let the animals stand until the drivers have had their breakfast. These same people then wonder why their stock are losing weight every day. No wonder that there are so many fatalities among saddle and pack animals when they are pushed too fast, too long, and too high in the wilderness!

Keeping Stock in Condition Some haywire packers forget to take stock salt and enough pellets or oats along for a couple of good feeds each day. Pellets and grain should be packed along with other supplies, especially in late fall when forage in the backcountry is badly frosted. It pays to take grain during the summer jaunts for small feeds for the hard working wrangling horse, and for the rest of the stock in the morning.

Forage Problems in the Backcountry Some outfitters pack hay and grain into their hunting camps in advance of opening day, thereby saving precious time early each morning in not having to wrangle stock that has been turned out to graze the night before. Others just carry enough "catch grain" to enable them to apprehend the animals. It is necessary to carry "pellet feed" in several sections of the 2,350 mile Pacific Crest Trail where grazing or pasturage is non-existent, and in several other areas of high rocky terrain.

The Wrangling or Camp Horse An outfitter or private party that turns his stock loose each night to graze generally keeps a wrangling horse picketed out near camp to enable him to gather the saddle and pack stock in the morning. The rest of the animals are belled and hobbled to graze at will. A mare is usually belled and the likely strayers hobbled.

Hobbling If you are a loner or with a small party, and own your own animals, you don't want your stock tied up all night because they need to feed, and you don't want to leave them loose because if you do you are not sure whether they will be feeding near camp, or miles away, or headed for the home corral in the morning. So you hobble the likely strayers, and the rest of the stock will usually stay near those so restricted. But hobbles have their disadvantages, too. If used ex-

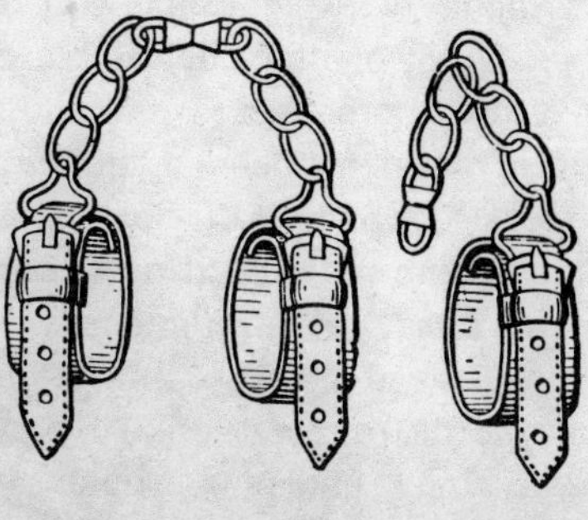

Double hobble (left) and picket hobble (right).

tensively, or improperly attached, they can make an animal's pasterns sore and stiff. Moreover, a horse or mule can become so accustomed to hobbles that he can learn to travel fairly well with them and he will travel a long way off during the night. I have seen horses that could be quite speedy when hobbled if a bunch of horses got to running. In one case, I had to hike five miles after one such animal who followed a pack string that was passing through the area to another camp.

Bell-Mare If you own or handle mostly mules, it is a good idea to keep a good bell-mare with your pack string, as it can make wrangling much easier. Mules seem to like to stick close to a mare. There will be less hunting for strays and homesick animals as long as you keep a belled mare from straying, and she won't stray if she is broken to picket. It's a wonderful feeling when you can wake up in the morning and hear that old cow-bell jangling nearby, and are greeted by a chorus of mules braying. Then it's just a matter of going out with a little catch oats to bring the pack string in.

Sacking Them Out! It can be downright dangerous and will give you an uneasy feeling to be astride a mount that is liable to explode and bolt every time a piece of paper, weed, or other debris blows across the trail in front of him. Perhaps it is your slicker or manty end that flaps or rustles as the pack animal moves close to brush or rocks along the trail. Sometimes a tie rope will accidentally come unfastened or a lead rope catch under the animal's tail, causing the animal to panic.

I recall that years ago my horse *Tia Jauna* would take off every time he heard a rattlesnake buzz up in the rocks as I rode along, and it was quite a job to gain control of him at some distance down the trail.

If your saddlehorse or one of the pack animals stampedes among a pack string it is going to cause havoc with the pack train and spread it all over the landscape and into all kinds of entanglements.

A Cure for Bolting It only takes a little patience and understanding to cure bolting before a safari, using what is called "The Running M," and with the assistance of a quiet and even-tempered friend who knows how to use it. Before you ever attempt sacking out an animal, have an experienced hand show you how it is applied. Generally, a surcingle rig with two rings at both sides of the bottom is used, along with a foot strap on each front foot to which a ring is attached. A rope is strung through this rigging, so that every time the animal attempts to bolt its front feet are pulled out from under it.

First, make sure that there are no stones or hard objects that may injure the animal when he is brought down to his knees. I have used knee pads on mounts that I have sacked.

A good helper on the trip-line will know when to take the feet out from under the animal, and when to let him up again. Even if he is sweating and snorting, he will stand no matter how many times you flap him with a blanket or sack after a few drops in this manner.

Morral Training If you or your wrangler have to chase all over the woods to catch your grazing stock, or fight your saddle horse or pack mule's head to get him bridled or haltered, you might try training him to using the morral. This simple piece of feeding equipment just might be the thing to make that old pony or pack mule walk right up to you when you need him. I know—it has worked for me for years!

The Morral I personally prefer the old U. S. Army type, since it is easier for the animal to breathe while eating and waste is nil. Nevertheless, there are regular commercial types on the market, both canvas and

U.S. Army horse feed bag.

leather. In an emergency many packers make morrals out of gunnysacks. You just cut the open end of the burlap sack down each side, leaving a two or three inch strip about 20 inches long. The flaps are folded back, the uncut sack part is filled with a quart or so of oats, and the strips are tied over the animal's poll. When you cut the sack, leave the flaps intact so that they may be folded over. The sack must be cut so that the animal's eyes are fully exposed. The morraly sacks can be discarded when needed no more.

The Advantages of the Morral Feeding stock from a morral has several advantages. Animals associate the tying on of a morral with something to eat, and therefore you will seldom find a morral-broken horse or mule that is head-shy or hard to halter or bridle. They will usually come to the morral when they see it and can even be led by it. Animals trained in this manner will generally come to, and not shy away from, a man with a halter or bridle in hand.

Gentle cooperation will get him on the trailer.

A sack morral on a strange horse is always tied with a single turn, so that if the animal takes off, the sack will fall off in a short distance.

An animal should not be turned loose with a morral on where it can get to water. When it attempts to drink the bag will fill with water, and the animal may drown. With the Army type, this is not possible.

Trailer Tips Loading and getting your mount through heavy traffic to the roadend or wherever you are taking him can be an ordeal for both you and the horse if he isn't trailer-broken. It can be a very frightening experience for the animal, especially if he has ever been in a trailer mishap or has some other unfortunate experience in his background. Here are a few tips that may be helpful.

Type of Trailer Is it a one stall or a two stall outfit? Many trailers are built with a standard six foot two inch height. You had better check and see what your horse's height is! He may not be able to stand comfortably if the roof is too low. This is something to be considered when purchasing a trailer, new or used. Most two-horse trailers are available with an extra four inches of height, and it may be worth an extra additional cost for safety reasons and for the comfort of your mount. If the horse isn't comfortable you can be in for some rough reactions.

No Experience If the animal has had no experience with a horse trailer, either good or bad, he still can be afraid of it, but for a different reason: fear of the unknown. You, of course, can get better cooperation from your horse if you are quiet and gentle with words and actions. Many animals have been injured or have become soured on these unstable wheeled platforms because the trainer was in too much of a hurry. Attempting to win a tug-of-war with a horse or mule that outweighs you many times over can be a losing proposition. *Don't* take a chance on rope burns or other injuries for either you or the horse! *Don't* try loading the first day or so!

Corral Training Try this: leave the trailer in the corral or pasture for a few days so that the animal(s) can see, smell, and inspect it. Be sure that the wheels are securely chocked so that the trailer is steady if an animal brushes up against it. In a couple of days, tie the horse to be hauled to the ring-bolt provided for that purpose at the end side of most trailers for an hour or two for several days.

Leave the tail-gate ramp down on the ground and put hay and grain in the trailer feed box. It is also wise to put a good nonskid floor mat in the trailer. That way, the footing will feel firm when he investigates what is inside this strange vehicle, and the sound of his steel-shod hoofs on the floor will be deadened and not so apt to spook him. Most animals eventually will

Loading mules and saddlehorse at the Redwood Ranger Station remount depot, Siskiyou National Forest, Oregon. (U.S. Forest Service photo.)

investigate how to get at the feed in the box, and when they decide that there aren't any horse-spooks inside to harm them, your troubles are nearly over.

Loading First be sure that your towing vehicle and horse trailer are in excellent condition. You don't want any breakdowns on the way to the roadend or wherever you are heading to unload your animal. Make sure that your towing vehicle is in gear with the brake on so that it will not roll forward or backward. Play it safe and chock the wheels of both car and trailer. Make certain that the trailer is securely hitched to the towing vehicle and that the safety chain is properly hooked up. The trailer wheels should be chocked and braced solidly so that the front end doesn't flip up when the animal steps on the rear end. Check well in advance of leaving that all equipment you will be using is in good repair and strong enough to do the job so that a break is unlikely. It can be downright annoying to have a tie rope or halter break when a spooky animal is half way into the rig.

The tailgate ramp should reach the ground, so that the animal doesn't have to step up onto it. If for any reason the ramp doesn't lie flat on the ground, move the trailer into a depression in the ground so that it does.

Whenever possible, try to load in a completely fenced in area. This way, if the horse does spook and break loose, he can't take off over into the next county.

Foot Lifting If the horse doesn't seem really afraid when you load him, but is a little hesitant about entering, you can sometimes help him by picking up one front foot at a time and setting it on the trailer ramp and on up into the trailer floor. Let him feel the trailer underfoot. Take your time. Keep cool—and by no means get impatient.

A truckload of mules and saddlehorse about ready to depart. (U.S. Forest Service photo.)

A Loading Problem One problem you may run into when using a two stall outfit is keeping the animal in line in position to load. There is no way to keep a horse or mule from walking in half circles all around the back of a stock trailer if he wants to. To help prevent this, you can use two ropes, 15 to 20 feet long. Tie one end to the center post of the trailer stall and the other end to the outside of the stall you are going to load him in, then lay the lines out straight behind the trailer. If your trailer has an escape door, it should be opened and ready for a quick exit if it becomes necessary. A second handler holds the two ropes, one on either side of the animal, much as you would use driving lines. With most animals, the added control of a rope lane right into the stall is enough to get them loaded without too much difficulty. You can use the same method with a one stall trailer. Tie the ropes to the outside ring-bolts on each side of the trailer, and proceed as outlined above.

The Tie-In Some well-trained animals may not need to be tied during transportation, but those that do should be tied with a hitch that will not jam and which can be unfastened with a quick jerk on the bitter or free end. Some horses that have not been trailered before may need to have their heads tied to keep them from getting caught with their heads bent backward.

Need of a Butt-Bar Some horses and mules tend to lean back against the butt-chain, bracing their feet hard forward, and putting most of their weight in the rear of the trailer well behind the axle. This tends to lift the weight off the tongue and may even put an up-load on the hitch, which will be dangerous. I use a piece of iron pipe as a butt bar instead of a chain because it rides against the muscle of the back of the horse's legs and is more comfortable for him to lean against. It won't hurt him, just encourages him to stand on all four feet, and tends to make him keep his weight properly forward.

Trailer Stalls Some stalls are not overly wide and many animals have a natural tendency to brace themselves with their feet further apart than the width of the stall allows when trailering. They just can't seem to find a comfortable and secure stance, and will sometimes panic and try to kick out the sides of the stall or attempt to climb over the walls looking for more room. Generally, this only occurs with one stall trailers. With a two stall trailer you might remove the solid divider, and replace it with a chain or pipe bar.

On Long Hauls Try to unload the animal for exercise every three or four hours. If possible, unload along a grassy spot so that the animals can graze and get a rest from the wheeled monster for a short period.

Watch out for roadsides that have been sprayed with poisonous weed killers!

Don't Upset Your Horse! A hair-rising ride in a trailer, jack-rabbit starts, and panic stops can make a nervous wreck out of your horse! If you don't give him a smooth steady ride on the way to a horse show or trail ride, you will certainly find that when it is time to reload for the return trip home "old Dobbin" will have turned into a bronc that regards the trailer monster with a jaundiced eye, and he will rebel or kick the hell out of the trailer demon! So plan ahead, drive carefully and cautiously. Remember that it takes longer to pass other traffic when towing a trailer with a heavy animal inside it. Watch out that the trailer doesn't get to swaying from side to side or you will have a sick horse—horses can get car sick too! Some owners forget that the horse or mule is flesh and blood and has feelings too!

Carry a Broom, Shovel and Axe These tools should be attached to all horse trailers so that the trailer floor can be kept clean and chocks can be cut for wheel blocks, unless you have chock blocks already cut.

Bibliography

The following books and magazines may be obtained from your local book store or your city or county library.

Anderson, Clarence W. *The Complete Book of Horses and Horsemanship*, Macmillan and Co., New York.

Back, Joe. *Horses, Hitches, and Rocky Trails*, Sage Books, Chicago; $2.95.

Brady, Irene. *America's Horses and Ponies*, Houghton Mifflin Co., New York; $7.50.

Conn, George H. *How to Get a Horse and Live With It*, Arco Publishing Co., New York; $10.00.

Denhart, Robert M. *Quarter Horses*, University of Oklahoma Press, Norman, Oklahoma; $5.95.

Gorman, John A. *The Western Horse*, Interstate Printers and Publishers, Danville, Illinois.

Griffith, Frank B. and Rubye Mae. *The Fun of Raising a Colt*, Arco Publishing Co., New York; $5.95.

Griffith, Frank B. and Rubye Mae. *How to Live With a Horse*, Arco Publishing Co., New York; $4.95.

Hawkins and Hummell Publications. *The Appaloosa Breed*; $5.00.

Hayes, M. Horace. *Points of the Horse*, Arco Publishing Co., New York; $12.50.

Hayes, M. Horace. *Veterinary Notes for Horse Owners*, revised by J. F. Donald Tutt, Arco Publishing Co., New York; $15.00.

Jones, Dave. *Practical Western Training*, Arco Publishing Co., New York; $5.95.

Jones, Dave. *The Western Trainer*, Arco Publishing Co., New York; $8.95.

Jones, William E., DVM, and Bogart, Robert, Ph.D. *Genetics of the Horse*, Caballus Publishing Co., Fort Collins, Colorado; $15.00.

Nye, Nelson C. *The Complete Book of the Quarter Horse*, Arco Publishing Co., New York; $15.00.

Phillips, Lance. *The Saddle Horse*, Arco Publishing Co., New York; $7.50.

Pittenger, Peggy Jett. *The Back-Yard Horse*, Arco Publishing Co., New York; $7.50.

Pittenger, Peggy Jett. *Morgan Horses*, Arco Publishing Co., New York; $7.50.

Ricci, James. *Understanding and Training Horses*, J. B. Lippincott Co., New York; $5.50.

Self, Margaret Cabell. *The Horseman's Encyclopedia*, Arco Publishing Co., New York; $9.75.

Self, Margaret Cabell. *Horsemastership*, Arco Publishing Co., New York; $8.50.

Self, Margaret Cabell. *Horses, Their Selection, Care, and Handling*, Arco Publishing Co., New York; $5.95.

Summerhays, R. S. *The Problem Horse*, Arco Publishing Co., New York; $4.95.

Straiton, E. C. *Horse Owner's Vet Guide*, J. B. Lippincott Co., New York; $8.95.

Vischer, Peter, editor. *Horse and Horseman*, Arco Publishing Co., New York; $14.95.

Williamson, Charles O. *Breaking and Training the Stock Horse*, The Williamson School of Horsemanship, P.O. Box 506, Hamilton, Montana; $7.50.

Wiseman, Robert F. *The Complete Horseshoeing Guide*, University of Oklahoma Press, Norman, Oklahoma; $4.95.

Wynmalen, Henry. *Dressage*, Arco Publishing Co., New York; $7.95.

Young, John Richard. *The Schooling of the Western Horse*, Univ. of Oklahoma Press; $6.95.

The Art and Science of Horsemanship, J. B. Lippincott Co., New York.

The Complete Book of Horses and Ponies, McGraw-Hill Publishing Co., New York; $5.95.

Going Light With Backpack or Burro, Sierra Club Books, New York; $2.75.

Books Available from the Western Horseman

The following books may be obtained from *The Western Horseman* Magazine, 3850 North Nevada Avenue, Colorado Springs, Colorado 80901 for $2.00 each:

Advanced Western Horsemanship
Beginning Western Horsemanship
Calf Roping
Games on Horseback
Health Problems of the Horse
Horse Breaking
Horseman's Scrap Book Volume 1
Horseman's Scrap Book Volume 2
Horseman's Scrap Book Volume 3
Horseman's Veterinarian Guide
Horsemen Through Civilization
Horseshoeing and Hoof Care
Intermediate Western Horsemanship
Rodeo Pictures
Training and Riding the Cutting Horse
Team Roping and Team Tying

Western Horseman magazine is available at $5.00 for a year's subscription.

Horse Book Club

The Horsemen's Book Society, 219 Park Avenue South, New York, New York 10003 offers a large selection of titles to members at considerable savings over the list price, including:

The Thoroughbred by E. S. Montgomery; Regular price $15.00, Member's price $10.50.

Riding and Training by Earl R. Farshler; Regular price $7.95, Member's price $6.95.

Horses and Horsemanship by Louise Evelyn Walraven; Regular price $8.50, Member's price $6.95.

Commonsense Horsemanship by Captain Vladimir S. Littauer, Regular price $8.95, Member's price $7.95.

Your Western Horse, His Ways and His Rider by Nelson C. Nye; Regular price $7.50, Member's price $5.95.

Horseman's Veterinary Advisor by Joseph B. Davidson, D.V.M.; Regular price $7.50, Member's price $6.50.

Your Horse and You by Heather Smith Thomas; Regular price $8.95, Member's price $6.95.

Other Interesting Outdoor Books

All About Camping by W. K. Merrill, District Park Ranger. All types of camping, hiking, horse care, hitches, and packing. Stackpole Books, Cameron & Kelker Streets, Harrisburg, Pennsylvania 17105; $3.95.

The Hunter's Bible by W. K. Merrill. Doubleday & Co., New York; $2.50.

The Hiker's & Backpacker's Handbook by W. K. Merrill. Hiking, mountaineering, and backpacking with pack stock. Arco Publishing Co., New York; $2.95.

The Survival Handbook by W. K. Merrill. Arco Publishing Co., New York; $1.95.

Bears in My Kitchen by Margaret Rose Merrill. McGraw-Hill Co., New York; $4.95.

APPENDIX

National Forests, Parks, Monuments, & Recreaton Areas

ALABAMA

William B. Bankhead National Forest, Box 40, Montgomery 36101
Conecuh National Forest, Box 40, Montgomery 36101
Horseshoe Bend National Military Park, Box 608, Dadeville 36853
Natchez Trace Parkway, Box 948, Tupelo, Mississippi (sections of parkway also located in Tennessee and Mississippi)
Russell Cave National Monument, Bridgeport 35740
Talladega National Forest, Box 40, Montgomery 36101
Tuskegee National Forest, Box 40, Montgomery 36101

ALASKA

Chugach National Forest, 328 E. 4th Ave., Anchorage 99501
Glacier Bay National Monument, Box 1781, Juneau 99801
Katmai National Monument, c/o Mt. McKinley National Park, McKinley Park 99755
Mt. McKinley National Park, McKinley Park 99755
Sitka National Monument, Box 1781, Juneau 99801

North Tongass National Forest, 217 2nd St., Juneau 99801

South Tongass National Forest, Box 2278, Ketchikan 99901

ARIZONA

Apache National Forest, Springerville 85938

Canyon de Chelly National Monument, Box 8, Chinle 86503

Casa Grande Ruins National Monument, Box 518, Coolidge 85228

Chiricahua National Monument, Dos Cabezas Star Route, Wilcox 85643

Coconino National Forest, 114 N. San Francisco St., Flagstaff 86002

Coronado National Forest, Post Office Building, Tucson 85702

Coronado National Memorial, Star Route, Hereford 85615

Glen Canyon National Recreation Area, Box 1507, Page 86040 (part of area located in Utah)

Grand Canyon National Park, Box 129, Grand Canyon 86023

Grand Canyon National Monument, c/o Grand Canyon National Park, Box 129, Grand Canyon 86023

Kaibab National Forest, 107 N. Second St., Williams 86046

Lake Mead National Recreation Area, 601 Nevada Highway, Boulder City, Nevada 89005 (part of area located in Nevada)

Montezuma Castle National Monument, Box 218, Camp Verde 86322

Navajo National Monument, Tonalea 86044

Organ Pipe Cactus National Monument,
Box 38, Ajo 85321

Petrified Forest National Park, Holbrook 86025

Pipe Spring National Monument,
Springdale, Utah 84767

Prescott National Forest, 344 S. Cortez St.,
Prescott 86301

Suguaro National Monument, Route 8, Box 350,
Tucson 85710

Sitgreaves National Forest, 113 W. Hopi Dr.,
Holbrook 86025

Susan Crater National Monument, c/o Wupatki
National Monument, Tuba Star Route,
Flagstaff 86003

Tonto National Forest, 230 N. First Ave., Room 6208,
Phoenix 85025

Tonto National Monument, Box 1088, Roosevelt 85545

Tumacacori National Monument, Box 67,
Tumacacori 85640

Tuzigoot National Monument, Box 36,
Clarksdale 86324

Walnut Canyon National Monument, Route 1,
Box 790, Flagstaff 86001

Wupatki National Monument, Tuba Star Route,
Flagstaff 86001

ARKANSAS

Arkansas Post National Memorial, c/o Hot Springs
National Park, Box 1219, Hot Springs 71902

Fort Smith National Historic Site, Box 1406,
Fort Smith 72902

Hot Springs National Park, Box 1219,
Hot Springs 71902

Ouachita National Forest, Box 1270,
Hot Springs 71902
Ozark and St. Francis National Forests, Forest Service Building, Russellville 72801
Pea Ridge National Military Park, Pea Ridge 72751

CALIFORNIA

Angeles National Forest, 1015 N. Lake St., Pasadena 91104
Cabrillo National Monument, Box 6175, San Diego 92106
Channel Islands National Monument, Box 6175, San Diego 92106
Cleveland National Forest, 1196 Broadway, San Diego 92101
Death Valley National Monument, Death Valley 92328 (portion of area also in Nevada)
Devils Postpile National Monument, Box 577, Yosemite National Park 95389
Eldorado National Forest, Placerville 95667
Inyo National Forest, 207 W. South St., Bishop 93514
Joshua Tree National Monument, Box 875, Twentynine Palms 92277
Kings Canyon National Park, Three Rivers 93271
Klamath National Forest, Yreka 96097
Lassen National Forest, Susanville 96130
Lassen Volcanic National Park, Mineral 96063
Lava Beds National Monument, Box 867, Tulelake 96134
Los Padres National Forest, Federal Building, Santa Barbara 93101
Mendocino National Forest, Willows 95988

Modoc National Forest, Alturas 96101
Muir Woods National Monument, Mill Valley 94943
Pinnacles National Monument, Paicines 95043
Plumas National Forest, Quincy 95971
Point Reyes National Seashore, Point Reyes 94956
San Bernardino National Forest, 175 West 5th Street, San Bernardino 92401
Sequoia National Forest, Porterville 93258
Sequoia National Park, Three Rivers 93271
Shasta-Trinity National Forest, 1615 Continental St., Redding 96001
Sierra National Forest, 4831 E. Shield Ave., Fresno 93726
Six Rivers National Forest, 331 J St., Eureka 95501
Stanislaus National Forest, Sonora 95370
Tahoe National Forest, Nevada City 95959
Toiyabe National Forest, 1555 South Wells Ave., Reno, Nevada 89502
Yosemite National Park, Box 577, Yosemite 95389

COLORADO

Arapaho National Forest, 1010 Tenth St., Golden 80402
Bent's Old Fort National Historic Site, Box 581, LaJunta 81050
Black Canyon of the Gunnison National Monument, c/o Curecanti National Recreation Area, Montrose 81401
Colorado National Monument, c/o Curecanti National Recreation Area, Montrose 81401
Dinosaur National Monument, Artesia 81610 (part of area located in Utah)

Grand Mesa-Uncompahgre National Forests, Delta 81416

Great Sand Dunes National Monument, Box 60, Alamosa 81101

Gunnison National Forest, Columbine Hotel, Gunnison 81230

Hovenweep National Monument, c/o Mesa Verde National Park 81330 (part of area located in Utah)

Mesa Verde National Park, Mesa Verde 81330

Pike National Forest, Post Office Building, Colorado Springs 80901

Rio Grande National Forest, Fassett Building, Monte Vista 81144

Rocky Mountain National Park, Box 1080, East Park 80517

Roosevelt National Forest, Post Office Building, Fort Collins 80522

Routt National Forest, Hunt Building, Steamboat Spring 80477

San Isabel National Forest, Pueblo 81002

San Juan National Forest, West Building, Durango 81301

Shadow Mountain National Recreation Area, c/o Rocky Mountain National Park, Box 1080, Estes Park 80517

White River National Forest, Glenwood Springs 81601

DISTRICT OF COLUMBIA

Battleground National Cemetery, National Capital Region, National Park Service, Washington 20242

House Where Lincoln Died National Memorial,

National Capital Region, National Park Service, Washington 20242

Lincoln Memorial National Memorial, National Capital Region, National Park Service, Washington 20242

Lincoln Museum National Memorial, National Capital Region, National Park Service, Washington 20242

National Capital Parks, National Capital Region, National Park Service, Washington 20242 (also areas in Maryland and Virginia)

Pennsylvania Avenue National Historic Site, c/o National Capital Parks

Thomas Jefferson National Memorial, National Capital Region, National Park Service, Washington 20242

Washington Monument National Memorial, National Capital Region, National Park Service, Washington 20242

White House National Capital Region, National Park Service, Washington 20242

FLORIDA

Apalachicola National Forest, Box 1050, Tallahassee 32302

Castillo de San Marcos National Monument, 1 Castillo Drive, St. Augustine 32084

De Soto National Memorial, Box 1377, Bradenton 33506

Everglades National Park, Box 279, Homestead 33030

Fort Caroline National Memorial, 1 Castillo Dr., St. Augustine 32084

Fort Jefferson National Monument, c/o Everglades National Park, Box 279, Homestead 33030

Fort Matanzas National Monument, 1 Castillo Dr., St. Augustine 32084
Ocala National Forest, Box 1050, Tallahassee 32302
Osceola National Forest, Box 1050, Tallahassee 32302

GEORGIA

Chattahoochee National Forest, P. O. Box 643, Gainesville 30501
Chickamauga and Chattanooga National Military Park, Fort Oglethorpe 30742 (part of park in Tennessee)
Fort Frederica National Monument, Box 816, St. Simons Island 31522
Fort Pulaski National Monument, Box 98, Savannah Beach 31328
Kennesaw Mountain National Battlefield Park, Box 1167, Marietta 30061
Ocmulgee National Monument, Box 4186, Macon 31208
Oconee National Forest, P. O. Box 643, Gainesville 30501

HAWAII

City of Refuge National Historical Park, Honaunau, Kona, Hawii 96726
Haleakala National Park, Box 456, Kahului, Maui 96732
Hawaii Volcanoes National Park, Hawaii 96718

IDAHO

Boise National Forest, 210 Main St., Boise 83702
Caribou National Forest, 427 North Sixth Ave., Pocatello 83201

Challis National Forest, Challis 83226
Clearwater National Forest, Orofino 83544
Coeur d'Alene National Forest, Coeur d'Alene 83814
Craters of the Moon National Monument, Box 29, Arco 83213
Kaniksu National Forest, Sandpoint 83864
Kootenai National Forest, Libby, Montana 59923
Nezperce National Forest, Grangeville 83530
Payette National Forest, McCall 83638
Salmon National Forest, Salmon 83467
Sawtooth National Forest, 1525 Addison Avenue East, Twin Falls 83301
St. Joe National Forest, St. Maries 83861
Targhee National Forest, St. Anthony 83445
Yellowstone National Park, Yellowstone Park, Wyoming 83020 (sections of park also in Wyoming and Montana)

ILLINOIS

Chicago Portage National Historic Site (not owned by the Federal Government), Superintendent, Cook County Forest Preserve, Cummings Square, River Forest
Shawnee National Forest, Harrisburg National Bank Building, Harrisburg 62946

INDIANA

Hoosier National Forest, Stone City National Bank Building, Bedford 47421
Lincoln Boyhood National Memorial, Lincoln City 47552

IOWA

Effigy Mounds, National Monument, Box K, McGregor 52157
Herbert Hoover National Historic Site, West Branch

KENTUCKY

Abraham Lincoln Birthplace National Historic Site, Route 1, Hodgenville 42748
Cumberland National Forest, Winchester 40391
Cumberland Gap National Historical Park, Box 840, Middlesboro 40965 (sections of park also in Tennessee and Virginia)
Mammoth Cave National Park, Mammoth Cave 42259

LOUISIANA

Chalmette National Historical Park, Box 125, Arabi 70032
Kisatchie National Forest, Box 471, Alexandria 71302

MAINE

Acadia National Park, Box 338, Bar Harbor 04609
White Mountain National Forest, Federal Building, Laconia, New Hampshire 03246

MARYLAND

Antietam National Battlefield Site, Box 158, Sharpsburg 21782
Antietam National Cemetery, Box 158, Sharpsburg 21782

Chesapeake and Ohio Canal National Monument, 479 North Potomac Street, Hagerstown 21740 (portion of area in West Virginia)

Fort McHenry National Monument and Historic Shrine, Baltimore 21230

George Washington Memorial Parkway, c/o National Capital Region, National Park Service, Washington, D. C. 20242 (section of parkway in Virginia)

Hampton National Historic Site, c/o Fort McHenry National Monument, Baltimore 21230

Harpers Ferry National Historical Park, Box 117, Harpers Ferry, West Virginia 25425 (portion of area in West Virginia)

National Capital Parks, c/o National Capital Region, National Park Service, Washington, D. C. 20242 (also areas in District of Columbia, Virginia and West Virginia)

MASSACHUSETTS

Adams National Historic Site, 135 Adams St., Quincy 02169

Cape Code National Seashore, Box 428, Eastham 02642

Dorchester Heights National Historic Site (not owned by the Federal Government), c/o Department of Parks, Boston

Minute Man National Historical Park, Room 1400 Post Office and Courthouse Building, Boston 02109

Salem Maritime National Historic Site, Custom House, Derby St., Salem 01970

MICHIGAN

Hiawatha National Forest, Escanaba 49829
Huron National Forest, Cadillac 49601
Isle Royale National Park, 87 N. Ripley St., Houghton 49931
Manistee National Forest, Cadillac 49601
Ottawa National Forest, Ironwood 49938

MINNESOTA

Chippewa National Forest, Cass Lake 56633
Grand Portage National Monument, Box 666, Grand Marais 55604
Pipestone National Monument, Box 727, Pipestone 56164
Superior National Forest, Federal Building, Duluth 55801

MISSISSIPPI

Bienville National Forest, Box 1291, Jackson 39205
Brices Cross Roads National Battlefield Site, c/o Natchez Trace Parkway, Box 948, Tupelo 38802
Delta National Forest, Box 1291, Jackson 39205
De Soto National Forest, Box 1291, Jackson 39205
Holly Springs National Forest, Box 1291, Jackson 39205
Homochitto National Forest, Box 1291, Jackson 39205
Natchez Trace Parkway, Box 948, Tupelo (portions of parkway also in Alabama and Tennessee)
Tombigbee National Forest, Box 1291, Jackson 39205
Tupelo National Battlefield, c/o Natchez Trace Parkway, Box 948, Tupelo 38802

Vicksburg National Cemetery, Box 349,
Vicksburg 39181
Vicksburg National Military Park, Box 349,
Vicksburg 39181

MISSOURI

Clark National Forest, Rolla 65401
George Washington Carver National Monument,
Box 38, Diamond 64840
Jefferson National Expansion Memorial National
Historic Site, 11 N. 4th St., St. Louis 63102
Mark Twain National Forest, Springfield 65806
Wilson's Creek National Battlefield Park, c/o George
Washington Carver National Monument

MONTANA

Beaverhead National Forest, Dillon 59725
Big Hole National Battlefield, c/o Yellowstone
National Park, Wyoming 83020
Bitterroot National Forest, Hamilton 59840
Custer National Forest, Billings 59101
Custer Battlefield National Monument, Box 116,
Crow Agency 59022
Deerlodge National Forest, Butte 59701
Flathead National Forest, Kalispell 59901
Gallatin National Forest, Bozeman 59715
Glacier National Park, West Glacier 59936
Helena National Forest, Helena 59601
Kootenai National Forest, Libby 59923
Lewis and Clark National Forest, Great Falls 59401
Lolo National Forest, Missoula 59801

Yellowstone National Park, Yellowstone Park, Wyoming 83020 (portions of park in Wyoming and Idaho)

NEBRASKA

Chimney Rock National Historic Site (not owned by Federal Government), c/o Superintendent, Scotts Bluff National Monument, Box 427, Gering 69341

Homestead National Monument of America, Beatrice 68310

Nebraska National Forest, Post Office Building, Lincoln 68508

Scotts Bluff National Monument, Box 427, Gering 69341

NEVADA

Death Valley National Monument, Death Valley, California 92328 (portion of area in California)

Humboldt National Forest, Post Office Building, Elko 89901

Lake Mead National Recreation Area, 601 Nevada Highway, Boulder City 89005 (portion of area in Arizona)

Lehman Caves National Monument, Baker 89311

Toiyabe National Forest, 1555 South Wells Avenue, Reno 89502

NEW HAMPSHIRE

White Mountain National Forest, Federal Building, Laconia 03246

NEW JERSEY

Edison National Historic Site, Box 126, Orange 07051
Morristown National Historical Park, Box 759, Morristown 07960

NEW MEXICO

Aztec Ruins National Monument, Route 1, Box 101, Aztec 87410
Bandelier National Monument, Los Alamos 87544
Capulin Mountain National Monument, Box 94, Capulin 88414
Carlsbad Caverns National Park, Box 1598, Carlsbad 88220
Carson National Forest, Taos 87571
Chaco Canyon National Monument, Box 156, Bloomfield 87413
Cibola National Forest, 304 U. S. Courthouse, Albuquerque 87103
Coronado National Forest, Tucson, Arizona 85702
El Morro National Monument, Ramah 87321
Fort Union National Monument, Watrous 87753
Gila National Forest, 301 West College Avenue, Silver City 88061
Gila Cliff Dwellings National Monument, Box 1320, Silver City 88061
Gran Quivira National Monument, Route 1, Mountainair 87036
Lincoln National Forest, Alamogordo 88310
Santa Fe National Forest, 130 Capitol Pl., Santa Fe 87501
White Sands National Monument, Box 458, Alamogordo 88310

NEW YORK

Castle Clinton National Monument, c/o New York City National Park Service Group, 28 East 20th St., New York 10003

Federal Hall National Memorial, c/o New York City National Park Service Group, 28 East 20th St., New York 10003

Fire Island National Seashore, P. O. Box 229, Patchogue, Long Island 11773

General Grant National Memorial, c/o New York City National Park Service Group, 28 East 20th St., New York 10003

Home of Franklin D. Roosevelt National Historic Site, Hyde Park, Dutchess County 12538

St. Paul's Church National Historic Site (not owned by Federal Government), Rector, Corporation of St. Paul's Church, 859 S. Columbus Ave., Mount Vernon 10550

Sagamore Hill National Historic Site, Oyster Bay, Long Island 11771

Saratoga National Historical Park, Route 1, Box 113-C, Stillwater 12170

Statue of Liberty National Monument, c/o New York City National Park Service Group, 28 East 20th Street, New York 10003

Theodore Roosevelt Birthplace National Historic Site, c/o New York City National Park Service Group, 28 East 20th St., New York 10003

Vanderbilt Manison National Historic Site, Hyde Park, Dutchess County 12538

NORTH CAROLINA

Blue Ridge Parkway, Box 1710, Roanoke,

Virginia 24008 (portion of parkway also in Virginia)

Cape Hatteras National Seashore, Box 457, Manteo 27954

Croatan National Forest, Box 731, Asheville 28802

Fort Raleigh National Historic Site, Box 457, Manteo 27954

Great Smoky Mountains National Park, Gatlinburg, Tennessee 37738 (portion of area in Tennessee)

Guilford Courthouse National Military Park, Box 9145, Plaza Station, Greensboro 27408

Moores Creek National Military Park, Currie, Pender County 28435

Nantahala National Forest, Box 731, Ashville 28802

Pisgah National Forest, Box 731, Asheville 28802

Uwharrie National Forest, Box 731, Asheville 28802

Wright Brothers National Memorial, Box 457, Manteo 27954

NORTH DAKOTA

Theodore Roosevelt National Memorial Park, Medora 58645

OHIO

Mound City Group National Monument, Box 327, Chillicothe 45601

Perry's Victory and International Peace Memorial National Monument, Box 78, Put-in-Bay 43456

Wayne National Forest, Stone City National Bank Building, Bedford, Indiana 47421

OKLAHOMA

Ouachita National Forest, Box 1270, Hot Springs, Arkansas 71902
Platt National Park, Box 379, Sulphur 73086

OREGON

Crater Lake National Park, Box 7, Crater Lake 97604
Deschutes National Forest, Bend 97701
Fort Clatsop National Memorial, Box 604 FC, Astoria 97103
Fremont National Forest, Lakeview 97630
Malheur National Forest, Grant County Bank Building, John Day 97845
McLoughlin House National Historic Site (not owned by Federal Government), Curator, Oregon City 97045
Mt. Hood National Forest, P. O. Box 5241, Portland 97216
Ochoco National Forest, Bottero Building, Prineville 97754
Oregon Caves National Monument, Box 7, Crater Lake 97604
Rogue River National Forest, Medford 97501
Siskiyou National Forest, Grants Pass 97526
Siuslaw National Forest, Ash Building, Corvallis 97330
Umatilla National Forest, Pendleton 97801
Umpqua National Forest, Federal Office Building, Roseburg 97470
Wallowa-Whitman National Forests, Baker 97814
Willamette National Forest, Post Office Building, Eugene 97401
Winema National Forest, Klamath Falls 97601

PENNSYLVANIA

Allegheny National Forest, Warren 16365
Fort Necessity National Battlefield, Star Route, Box 15, Farmington 15437
Gettysburg National Cemetery, Gettysburg 17325
Gettysburg National Military Park, Gettysburg 17325
Gloria Dei (Old Swedes') Church National Historic Site (not owned by Federal Government), Rector, Delaware Avenue and Christian Street, Philadelphia
Hopewell Village National Historic Site, Route 1, Elverson 19520
Independence National Historical Park, 420 Chestnut St., Philadelphia 19106

RHODE ISLAND

Touro Synogogue National Historic Site (not owned by Federal Government), President, The Society of Friends of Touro Synogogue National Historic Shrine, Inc., 85 Touro St., Newport 02840

SOUTH CAROLINA

Cowpens National Battlefield Site, c/o Kings Mountain National Military Park, Box 31, Kings Mountain, North Carolina 28086
Fort Sumter National Monument, Box 428, Sullivan's Island 29482
Francis Marion National Forest, 901 Sumter St., Columbia 29201
Kings Mountain National Military Park, Box 31, Kings Mountain, North Carolina 28086

Sumter National Forest, 901 Sumter St.,
Columbia 29201

SOUTH DAKOTA

Badlands National Monument, Box 72, Interior 57750
Black Hills National Forest, Custer 57730
Jewel Cave National Monument, c/o Wind Cave
National Park, Hot Springs 57747
Mount Rushmore National Memorial, Keystone 57751
Wind Cave National Park, Hot Springs 57747

TENNESSEE

Andrew Johnson National Historic Site,
Greenville 37743
Cherokee National Forest, P. O. Box 400,
Cleveland 37312
Chickamauga and Chattanooga National Military Park,
Fort Oglethorpe, Georgia 30742 (portion
of area in Georgia)
Cumberland Gap National Historical Park, Box 840,
Middlesboro, Kentucky 40965 (portions of area
in Kentucky and Virginia)
Fort Donelson National Military Park, Box F,
Dover 37058
Fort Donelson National Cemetery, Box F, Dover 37058
Great Smoky Mountains National Park, Gatlinburg
37738 (portion of area in North Carolina)
Natchez Trace Parkway, Box 948, Tupelo, Mississippi
(parkway also located in Alabama and Mississippi)
Shiloh National Cemetery, Shiloh 38376
Shiloh National Military Park, Shiloh 38376

Stones River National Battlefield, Box 1039,
Murfreesboro 37131
Stones River National Cemetery, Box 1039,
Murfreesboro 37131

TEXAS

Angelina National Forest, Box 380, Lufkin 75902
Big Bend National Park, Big Bend 79834
Davy Crockett National Forest, Box 380, Lufkin 75902
Fort Davis National Historic Site, Box 785,
Fort Davis 70734
Padre Island National Seashore, P. O. Box 4012,
Corpus Christi 78408
Sabine National Forest, Box 380, Lufkin 75902
Sam Houston National Forest, Box 380, Lufkin 75902
San Jose Mission National Historic Site (not owned
by Federal Government), Manager, San Jose
Mission National Historic Site, 6519 San Jose Dr.,
San Antonio 78214

UTAH

Arches National Monument, c/o Canyonlands
National Park, Uranium Bldg., Moab 84532
Ashley National Forest, Vernal 84078
Bryce Canyon National Park, Bryce Canyon 84717
Cache National Forest, Post Office Building,
Logan 84321
Canyonlands National Park, Uranium Bldg., Moab,
Utah 84532
Capitol Reef National Monument, Torrey 84775
Caribou National Forest, 427 North Sixth Ave.,
Pocatello, Idaho 83201

Cedar Breaks National Monument, c/o Zion National Park, Springdale 84767

Dinosaur National Monument, Artesia, Colo. 81610 (portion of area in Colorado)

Dixie National Forest, Cedar City 84720

Fishlake National Forest, Richfield 84701

Glen Canyon National Recreation Area, Box 1507, Page, Arizona 86040 (portion of area in Arizona)

Golden Spike National Historic Site (not owned by Federal Government), President, Golden Spike Association of Box Elder County, Brigham City, Utah 84302

Hovenweep National Monument, c/o Mesa Verde National Park, Colorado 81330 (portion of monument in Colorado)

Manti-La Sal National Forest, 350 East Main St., Price 84501

Natural Bridges National Monument, c/o Arches National Monument, Box 98, Moab 84532

Rainbow Bridge National Monument, c/o Navajo National Monument, Tonalea, Arizona 86044

Timpanogos Cave National Monument, Route 1, Box 200, American Fork 84003

Uinta National Forest, Provo 84601

Wasatch National Forest, 430 South 4th St. East, Salt Lake City 84111

Zion National Park, Springdale 84767

VERMONT

Green Mountain National Forest, 22 Evelyn St., Rutland 05701

VIRGINIA

Appomattox Court House National Historical Park, Box 218, Appomattox 24522

Blue Ridge Parkway, Box 1710, Roanoke 24008 (Portion of area in North Carolina)

Booker T. Washington National Monument, Route 1, Box 194, Hardy 24101

Colonial National Historical Park, Box 210, Yorktown 23490

Cumberland Gap National Historical Park, Box 840, Middlesboro, Kentucky 40965 (portions of area in Tennessee and Kentucky)

Custis-Lee Mansion National Memorial, c/o National Capital Region, National Park Service, Washington, D. C. 20242

Fredericksburg National Cemetery, Box 679, Fredericksburg 22401

Fredericksburg and Spotsylvania County Battlefields Memorial National Military Park, Box 679, Fredericksburg 22401

George Washington Birthplace National Monument, Washington's Birthplace 22575

George Washington Memorial Parkway, c/o National Capital Region, National Park Service, Washington D. C. 20242 (section of parkway in Maryland)

George Washington National Forest, Harrisonburg 22801

Jamestown National Historic Site (not owned by Federal Government), Association for Preservation of Virginia Antiquities, John Marshall House, 9th and Marshall Sts., Richmond 23219

Jefferson National Forest, 920 S. Jefferson St., Roanoke 24001
Manassas National Battlefield Park, Manassas 22110
National Capital Parks, c/o National Capital Region, National Park Service, Washington 20242 (areas also in District of Columbia and Maryland)
Petersburg National Battlefield, Box 549, Petersburg 23804
Poplar Grove (Petersburg) National Cemetery, c/o Petersburg National Battlefield, Box 549, Petersburg 23804
Richmond National Battlefield Park, 3215 E. Broad St., Richmond 23223
Shenandoah National Park, Luray 22835
Yorktown National Cemetery, c/o Colonial National Historical Park, Box 210, Yorktown 23490

WASHINGTON

Colville National Forest, Colville 99114
Coulee Dam National Recreation Area, Box 37, Coulee Dam 99116
Fort Vancouver National Historic Site, Vancouver 98661
Gifford Pinchot National Forest, 1408 Franklin St., Vancouver, 98661
Mount Baker National Forest, Bellingham 98225
Mount Rainier National Park, Longmire 98397
Okanogan National Forest, Okanogan 98840
Olympic National Forest, Post Office Building, Olympia 98501
Olympic National Park, 600 E. Park Ave., Port Angeles, 98362

Snoqualmie National Forest, 905 Second Ave. Building, Seattle 98104
Wenatchee National Forest, Wenatchee 98801
Whitman Mission National Historic Site, Route 2, Walla Walla 99362

WEST VIRGINIA

Chesapeake and Ohio Canal National Monument, 479 North Potomac St., Hagerstown 21740 (portion of area in Maryland)
Harpers Ferry National Historical Park, Box 117, Harpers Ferry 25425 (portion of area in Maryland)
Monongahela National Forest, Federal Building, Elkins 26241

WISCONSIN

Chequamegon National Forest, Park Falls 54552
Nicolet National Forest, Merchants State Bank Building, Rhinelander 54501

WYOMING

Bighorn National Forest, Columbus Building, Sheridan 82801
Black Hills National Forest, Custer, South Dakota 55730
Bridger National Forest, Kemmerer 83101
Caribou National Forest, 427 North Sixth Ave., Pocatello, Idaho 83201
Devils Tower National Monument, Devils Tower 82714

Fort Laramie National Historic Site, Fort Laramie 82212
Grand Teton National Park, Box 67, Moose 83012
Medicine Bow National Forest, Laramie 82071
Shoshone National Forest, Blair Office Building No. 1, Cody 82414
Teton National Forest, Jackson 73001
Yellowstone National Park, Yellowstone Park 83020 (portions of park in Idaho and Montana)

PUERTO RICO

Caribbean National Forest, Box 577, Rio Piedras 00928
San Juan National Historic Site, Box 712, San Juan 00902

VIRGIN ISLANDS

Buck Island Reef National Monument, c/o Virgin Islands National Park, Box 1707, Charlotte Amalie, St. Thomas 00802
Christiansted National Historic Site, c/o Virgin Islands National Park, Box 1707, Charlotte Amalie, St. Thomas 00802
St. Thomas National Historic Site, c/o Virgin Islands National Park, Box 1707, Charlotte Amalie, St. Thomas 00802
Virgin Islands National Park, Box 1707, Charlotte Amalie, St. Thomas 00802

NATIONAL FOREST REGIONAL HEADQUARTERS OFFICES

(Each offers a free booklet about recreational areas in that region)

Northern Region, Federal Building, Missoula, Montana 59801

Rocky Mountain Region, Denver Federal Center, Building 85, Denver, Colorado 80225

Southwestern Region, Federal Building, Albuquerque, New Mexico 87101

Intermountain Region, Forest Service Building, Ogden, Utah 84403

California Region, 630 Sansome St., San Francisco, California 94111

Pacific Northwest Region, P. O. Box 3623, Portland, Oregon 97212

Eastern Region, 6816 Market St., Upper Darby, Pennsylvania 19082

Southern Region, 50 Seventh St., N.E., Atlanta, Georgia 30323

North Central Region, 710 N. 6th St., Milwaukee, Wisconsin 53203

Alaska Region, Fifth St. Office Building, Juneau, Alaska 99801

NATIONAL PARK SERVICE

REGIONAL OFFICES

(Subject to supply and demand, individual requests for free booklets about areas in each Region will be honored by the Region in which the areas are located)

Southeast Regional Office, National Park Service,
Federal Building, Box 10008, Richmond,
Virginia 23240

Midwest Regional Office, National Park Service,
1709 Jackson St., Omaha, Nebraska 68102

Southwest Regional Office, National Park Service,
Box 728, Santa Fe, New Mexico 87501

Western Regional Office, National Park Service,
450 Golden Gate Ave., San Francisco,
California 94105

Northeast Regional Office, National Park Service,
143 South Third St., Philadelphia,
Pennsylvania 19106

Northwest Regional Office, National Park Service,
1424 Fourth Ave,
Seattle, Washington 98101

National Capital Regional Office, National Park Service,
1100 Ohio Dr., S.W., Washington, D. C. 20242

Address of the main office of the National Park Service:
National Park Service
Department of the Interior Building
Washington, D. C. 20240

BUREAU OF LAND MANAGEMENT
LAND OFICES

Alaska:
555 Cordova St.
Anchorage, Alaska 99501

516 Second Ave.
Fairbanks, Alaska 99701

Arizona:
Federal Bldg., Room 204
Phoenix, Ariz. 85025

California:
Federal Bldg., Room 4017
Sacramento, Calif. 95814
1414 Eighth St.
Riverside, Calif. 92502

Colorado:
14027 Federal Bldg.
Denver, Colo. 80202

Idaho:
323 Federal Bldg.
Boise, Idaho 83701

Montana:
(N. Dak., S. Dak.):
Federal Bldg.
316 North 26th St.
Billings, Mont. 59101

Nevada:
Federal Bldg., 300 Booth St.
Reno, Nev. 89505

New Mexico (Okla):
Federal Bldg.
Santa Fe, N. Mex. 87501

Oregon:
729 Northeast Oregon St.
Portland, Oreg. 97232

Utah:
Eighth Floor, Federal Bldg.
125 South State St.
P.O. Box 11505
Salt Lake City, Utah 84110

Washington:
729 Northeast Oregon St.
Portland, Oreg. 97232

Wyoming (Nebr., Kan.):
2120 Capitol Ave.
Cheyenne, Wyo. 82001

All Other States:
Robin Bldg.
7981 Eastern Ave.
Silver Spring, Md. 20910

Dealers and Outfitters

Listed Alphabetically by State

SYMBOLS: (A) Mountaineering and backpack equipment; (B) General camping and outdoor equipment; (C) Other specialties; * Catalog available.

ALASKA

Buness Brothers (B)
Wrangell, 99929

Hammer & Wikan (B)
Box 249
Petersburg, 99833

Rusher's Juneau Young Co. (B)
Juneau, 99801

Skinner's (B)
118 Seward
Juneau, 99801

ARIZONA

Cap Trails (C)
(Packs, tents)
3920 West Clarendon
Phoenix, 85019

CALIFORNIA

Abercrombie & Fitch (B)*
220 Post St.
San Francisco, 94108

Ames-Harris-Neville (B)
2800 17th St.
San Francisco, 94110

Antelope Camping Equipment (B)
10268 Imperial Ave.
Cupertino, 95514

Cutter Laboratories (Snakebite & Insect Kits
4th & Parker St.,
Berkeley, 94710

Gerry Mountain Sports (B)*
228 Grant St.
San Francisco, 95014

Highland Outfitters (B)*
3579 University Ave.
P. O. Box 121
Riverside, 92502

Himalayan Industries (C)*
(Pack frames, bags)
807 Cannery Row
P. O. Box 950
Monterey, 93940

Kelty Pack, Inc. (C)*
Mountaineer Packs
Victory Blvd.
P. O. Box 3453
Glendale, 91201

Sierra Mountain Equipment (A)
2211 California St.
P. O. Box 15251
San Francisco, 94115

Sports Chalet (A)*
951 Foothill Blvd.
P. O. Box 626
La Canada, 91011

The North Face (A)*
Alpine Equipment Specialists
308 Columbus Ave.
San Francisco, 94133

The North Face (A)*
700 Welch Rd.
Palo Alto, 94300
5 Country Club Plaza
Orinda, 94563
2804 Telegraph Ave.
Berkeley, 94705

The Ski Hut (Trailwise) (A)*
1615 University Ave.
Berkeley, 94703

Sierra Designs (C)*
4th & Addison Sts.
Berkeley, 94710

Swiss Ski Sports (B)
559 Clay St.
San Francisco, 94111

COLORADO

Alp Sport (C)
3245 Prairie Ave.
P. O. Box 1081
Boulder, 80302

Colorado Outdoors Sports (A)*
Gerry Division
5450 N. Valley Highway
Denver, 80216

Dave Cooks Sporting Goods (B)*
1603A Larimer St.
Denver, 80202

Gart Brothers (B)*
Sporting Goods Company
1643 Larimer St.
Denver, 80202

Holubar Mountaineering (A)*
Retail stores in Boulder, Denver
P. O. Box 7
Boulder, 80302

Sportsman Products (C)
Plastic snowshoes
P. O. Box 1082
Boulder, 80302

Survival Research Laboratories (A)*
Air-Land-Sea-Trail Survival Kits
17 Marland Rd.
Colorado Springs, 80906

Frostline Outdoor Equipment (C)*
Do-it-yourself kits
P. O. Box 1378
Boulder, 80302

ILLINOIS

Kien's Sporting Goods (B)*
227 W. Washington
Chicago, 60606

MAINE

L. L. Bean (B)*
278 Maine St.
Freeport, 04032

MARYLAND

Bishop's Outdoor Equipment (C)
6804 Millwood Rd.
Bethesda, 20034

H & H Surplus Center (B)*
Catalog 25 cents.
1028 West Baltimore
Baltimore, 21223

MASSACHUSETTS

Corcoran, Inc. (B)*
Stoughton, 02072

Don Gleason's Camper's Supply (B)*
Catalog 25 cents.
9 Pearl St.
Northampton, 01060

Moor & Mountain (B)
14 Main St.
Concord, 01742
Eastern Mountain Sports, Inc. (B)
1041 Commonwealth Ave.
Boston, 02215
Wellesley, 02181
Springfield, 01101

MINNESOTA

Gokey Company (B)*
21 West Fifth St.
St. Paul, 55102
Herter's Inc. (B)*
Catalog 50 cents.
Rural Route 1
Waseca, 56093

MISSOURI

Gateway Sporting Goods (B)*
3177 Mercier Street
Kansas City, 64111

NEW HAMPSHIRE

Peter Limmer & Sons (B)
Intervale, 03845

NEW JERSEY

Morsan — Outfitters (B)*
810 Route 17
Paramus, 07652
Farmingdale, N. Y., 11375

NEW YORK

Abercrombie & Fitch (B)*
Madison Ave. at 45th St.
New York, 10017
Thomas Black & Sons (B)*
Catalog 25 cents.
930 Ford St.
Ogdensburg, 13669
Camp & Trail Outfitters (A)*
Catalog 25 cents.
112 Chambers St.
New York, 10007
Gloy's (B)
11 Addison St.
Larchmont, 10538
Walter E. Stern (B)
254 Nagle Ave.
New York, 10034
Parker Distributors (B)
40 Industrial Place
New Rochelle, 10805
Mountaineering Supply (B)
897 St. David's Lane
Schenectady, 12309

OKLAHOMA

P & S Sales (B)*
P. O. Box 155
Tulsa, 74102

OREGON

Alaska Sleeping Bag Co. (A)*
701 N. W. Dawson Way
Beaverton, 97005
Alpine Hut (A)*
1250 Loyd Center
Portland, 97232
Norm Thomson (B)*
Outfitters
1805 N. W. Thurman
Portland, 97209

PENNSYLVANIA

I. Goldberg (B)*
429 Market St.
Philadelphia, 19106
Survival Equip. Co. (C)*
Berkes County,
Oley, 19547

TEXAS

B & S Outfitters (B)*
P. O. Box 8
Hooks, 75561

WASHINGTON

Alpine Hut, Inc. (A)*
2650 University Village
Seattle, 98105
Alpine Hut (A)*
420 Tacoma Mall
Tacoma, 98409
Alpine Hut (A)*
Renton Shopping Center
Renton, 98055
Alpine Hut, Inc. (A)*
Central Offices
Mail Order Division
4725 30th Ave. N. E.
Seattle, 98105
Eddie Bauer (A)*
Outfitter
417 East Pine St.
Seattle, 98122
Recreational Equipment Inc. (A)*
1525 11th Ave.
Seattle, 98122

WISCONSIN

Gander Mountain, Inc. (B)*
Outfitters
P. O. Box 248
Wilmot, 53192
Laacke & Joys Co. (B)*
1433 North Water St.
Milwaukee, 53202

DISTRICT OF COLUMBIA

The Trading Post (B)
3336 N. St.
Washington, D. C., 20004

CANADA

The T Eaton Company (B)
190 Yonge St.
Toronto, 1
Simpson-Sears Ltd. (B)
108 Mutual St.
Toronto, 2
Premier Cycle & Sports (B)
Mountaineering outfitters
319 Seventh Ave., S. W.
Calgary
Arlberg Sports Haus (B)
Outfitters
816 W. Pender St.
Vancouver, 1
Woodwards (B)
Hastings & Abbot St.
Vancouver, 3
Thomas Black & Sons (A)*
Catalog 25 cents.
225 Strathcona Ave.
Ottawa, 3

Sources of Emergency Rations & Dehydrated Foods

Ann Benedict's
Dri-Lite Foods
11333 Atlantic Ave.
Lynwood, Calif. 90262
Ad Seidel Trail Packets
1245 W. Dickens Ave.
Chicago, Ill. 60014
Bernard's Food Industries
(East of Rocky Mountains)
217 N. Jefferson St.
Chicago, Ill. 60606
(West of Rocky Mountains)
222 South 24th St.
P.O. Box 487
San Jose, Calif. 95103
(Canada)
120 Sunrise Ave.
Toronto, Ontario Canada
Chuck Wagon
Survival Food Packs
P.O. Box 66
Newton, Mass. 01355
Cramore Fruit Products
90 West Broadawy
New York, N.Y. 10007
E-Z Food Products Company
1420 So. Western Ave.
Gardena, Calif. 90247
Firefly Survival Rations
Coast Guard Type
Safety Research & Mfg. Co.
Seattle, Wash. 90104
H & M Packing Corporation
(Survival Packs 3-8-14 day kits)
915 Ruberta Ave.
Glendale, Calif. 91201
Lyon's Food Specials
P.O. Box 11215
Los Angeles, Calif. 90011
Mergen Industries
6808 Marshall Rd.
Upper Darby, Pa. 19082
Seidel Trail Packets
David Abercrombie Company
97 Chambers St.
New York, N.Y. 10007
Stow-A-Way Products
Survival Foods
Freeze-Dri & Dehydrated Foods
Cohasset, Mass. 02025
Trail Meals
J. B. Kisky
1829 N.E. Alberta St.
Portland, Ore. 97211
Trailwise Ski Hut
1615 University Ave.
Berkeley, Calif. 94702
Trip-Lites
S. Gumpett
812 Jersey Ave.
Jersey City, N. J. 07302
Tripperoos
Hilker & Bletsch
614 Hubbard St.
Chicago, Ill. 60609
Trail Feeding Specialties
Box 441
Summit, N. J. 07901
Survival Research Laboratories
17 Marland Rd.
Colorado Springs, Colo. 80906

Index

Acadia National Park, 30, 31
Alaska, 141
Alaska Highway, 142, 146, 147
all-expense jaunt, 43
American Donkey and Mule Society, 54
American Forestry Association, 77
Appalachian Trail, 27, 32
Arbuckle Reservoir, 29, 32
Arches National Monument, 29, 32
Arizona hitch, 166

backpacking, 45
Badlands National Monument, 29, 31
Bandelier National Monument, 32
barley, 234
bell mare, 248
Big Bend National Park, 32
Black Hills, 88
blind horses, 224
bloodworms, 207
Blue Ridge Parkway, 30, 31
Bob Marshal Wilderness Area, 25
bolting, cure for, 249
boots, 153
bowline knot, 127
bran, 235
breakfast, 182
Bright Angel Trail, 78
Bryce Canyon National Park, 32
buckskin horses, 224
burro, 52, 54
  feeding of, 229
  gear, 103
  grooming, 108
  handling, 105ff
  hobbling, 122
  picketing, 122
  safari, 93ff
  turning loose, 122
butt bar, 256

camp, procedure for arriving, 244
camp cookery, 179ff
camp cutlery, 184
camp horse, 247
camp kitchen gear, 183
camp oven, 184
campfire, 185
camping gear, 97
campsite, selecting, 118

Canadian Government Travel Bureau, 90
Canadian Pacific Railways, 90
Canadian provincial travel bureaus, 90, 91
Canyon de Chelly National Monument, 32
Canyonlands National Park, 32
catch grain, 126
Chattanooga National Military Park, 31
Chickamauga National Military Park, 31
Chief Joseph Trail, 84
Chiricahua National Monument, 32
Chugach National Forest, 143
cinch adjustment, 165
clothes, 91
coastal ranges, 25
Colorado, 82
Colorado National Park, 31
Continental Divide Trail, 27, 30
cooking time, 185
cooking utensils, 99
corn, 234
corral training, 252
Coulee Dam Recreation Area, 30, 32
Crater Lake National Park, 32
Curecanti Recreational Area, 29, 31

day trips, 48
dead stock, 205
Death Valley National Monument, 32, 82
Death Valley Trail, 82
Decker saddle, 170
dehydrated food, 188
Denali Highway, 143
Denali program, 132
De Soto, 22
Devils Postpile National Monument, 32
digestive system of pack animals, 232
Dinosaur National Monument, 29, 31
dude ranches, 75
dunnage pack, 44, 48

easy keeper, 218
extended pack safari, 43

fire, hunter's, 187
fire, keyhole, 187
fire permit, 185
fireplace, rock, 187
first aid, 189ff
first aid course, Red Cross, 195
first aid guide, US Forest Service, 197
first aid for mount, 198ff
food constituents, animal, 233
food storage suggestions, 193
Forest Products Laboratory, 38
Forest Rangers, 38
4-H Clubs, 24
fuel, 243

Gallatin National Park, 86
game refuges, 144
Gila Wilderness, 87
Glacier Bay National

Monument, 35, 144, 146
Glacier National Park, 28, 30, 31
Gold Rush Trails, 28
Grand Canyon National Park, 28, 29, 32, 54, 77
Grand Teton National Park, 30, 31
grasslands, 25
Great Northern Railway, 90
Great Smoky Mountain National Park, 31
grub list, 180
guest code of ethics, 136
guest ranches, 76

Haleakala National Park, 28, 32
Hawaii Volcanoes National Park, 32
hay, 236
High Sierra Nevadas of California, 25
horse
  bots, 210
  care of, 229ff
  feeding of, 229
  flu vaccine, 201
  foot care, 212
  selecting a, 215ff
  watering of, 229
  wrangling, 247
horseback riding, 28
hobbling, 247
Hot Springs National Park, 31
hunting, 92

Idaho, 84
Illinois, 84
immunization, 195
Indian pony, 224
Institute of Northern Forestry, 38
Institute of Tropical Forestry, 38

John Muir Trail, 79, 161
John Muir Wilderness, 79
Joshua Tree National Monument, 32

Kamp-pack envelopes, 190
Katmai National Monument, 144
Kings Canyon National Park, 82
kitchen gear, 180
kyacks, 240

lanterns, 243
Lassen Volcanic National Park, 32
Lewis and Clark Trail, 27
linseed meal, 235
loading of horses, 254
Los Angeles Equestrian Center, 24
lunch, 182

Marine Highway, 146
menu, 97
Mesa Verde National Park, 32
miles per day, 114
Missouri, 86
Mogollon Mountains, 87
Montana, 86
Morgan pack animals, 217
Mormon Battalion Trail, 28
morral, 249
Mount Forsaker, 144

Mount McKinley National Park, 143
Mount Rainer National Park, 32
mountain canary, 96
mule, 52, 54
  care of, 229ff
  feeding of, 229
  riding, 54
Multiple Use, 36

Natchez Trace National Parkway, 31
Natchez Trail, 27
National Capital Parks, 31
National Forest System, 7
National Forests, 11, 17, 25, 33
National Forests Trail System, 32
National Grasslands, 36
National Park Service, 33
National Park System, 28, 29, 31, 33, 36
National Parks, 11, 17, 33
National Rifle Association, 132
NRA Hunting Code of Ethics, 132
National Scenic Trail System, 27
National Scenic Trails, 30
National Wilderness Preservation System, 38
Navajo National Monument, 32
New Mexico, 87
North Country Trail, 27
Northern California Horseman's Association, 81
Northern Pacific Railway, 90

oats, 234
Old Cattle Trails, 27
Old Mormon Trail, 27
Olympic National Park, 30, 32
Olympic National Park's Rain Forest, 54
Oregon Trail, 27
Organ Pipe Cactus National Monument, 29, 32
outfitter's standards, 135
Ozark Mountains, 86

Pacific Coast Trail, 30
Pacific Crest Trail, 27, 247
Pacific Crest Trail System, 33, 79
pack
  bags, 240
  hitches, 170
  horse, selecting a, 220
  outfit, 75
  outfit checklist, 169
  station, contacting, 103
  trips, 42
packaged food, 242
packhorse hunting, 129ff
packing
  breakable items, 243
  canned goods, 243
  eggs, 242
  fresh meat, 243
  a riding saddle, 162
panniers, 240
pastures, 237
Pennsylvania, 87
permits, 104
pinto horses, 222
Platt National Park, 32
Point Reyes National Seashore, 32
Potomac Heritage Trail, 27

prairie lands, 25
pressure cooker, 184
pulse of horse, 225
Purina Horse Research Center, 231

Quarter Horse, 23

rabies, 199
Rainbow Bridge National Monument, 32
renting an animal, 218
rice, 235
Rocky Mountain National Park, 31
Rocky Mountains, 25
rye, 234

saddle
  Army McClellan, 160
  Decker pack, 156
  Phillips pack, 160
  riding, 153
  sawbuck, 155, 169
saddling up, 162
safari cost, 47
Saguaro National Monument, 32
salt, 236
Santa Fe Railway, 90
Santa Fe Trail, 27
Selway Wilderness Area, 25
Sequoia National Park, 82
Sequoia-King Canyon National Parks, 30, 32, 79
Shadow Mountain National Recreation Area, 32
Shenandoah National Park, 31
Sierra Club, The, 77
Sitka National Monument, 146
snake bite, 200
soundness examination, 215
South Dakota, 87
Southern Pacific Railway, 90
Spanish Conquistadores, 22
Spanish ponies, 224
spot trip, one-day, 42
spot trip, two-day, 42
State Game Wardens, 38
streams, fording, 118
supper, 183
Sustained Yield, 36

tack tent, 244
Targhee National Forest, 89
Texas, 22, 89
Theodore Roosevelt National Memorial Park, 32
Tongass National Forest, 143
trail rides, 42, 75
trailer stalls, 256
trial period, 216
tympanitic colic, 202

Union Pacific Railway, 90
US Bureau of Land Management, 18
US Department of Agriculture, 7, 23
US Department of Interior, 18
US Forest Service, 7
US Park Rangers, 38

Vermont Long Trail, 27
veterinarian, 206
volcanism, 144

Washington, D.C., 30
weight, calculating, 101
wheat, 235
Wilderness Act of 1964, 19
Wilderness Society, The, 77
Wyoming, 89

Yellowstone National Park, 30, 31, 35, 36, 86
Yosemite National Park, 30, 32, 79, 168

Zion National Park, 32